T0125011

VISIT TEEPEE TOWN

Native Writings After the Detours

VISIT TEEPEE TOWN

Native Writings
After the Detours

edited by Diane Glancy
and Mark Nowak

COFFEE HOUSE PRESS :: MINNEAPOLIS

COVER ART: Arthur Amiotte, "Prince Albert" / Minneapolis Institute of Arts
and Phil Young, "Visit Teepee Town"
BACK COVER ART: Phil Young, "Genuine Indian Quantum Card Box (detail 2)"
and Hachivi Edgar Heap of Birds, "New York: Purchased? Stolen? Reclaimed?"
BOOK + COVER DESIGN: Kelly N. Kofron

Please see pp. 361 – 372 for a list of contributors and acknowledgments.

Coffee House Press is an independent nonprofit literary publisher supported in
part by a grant provided by the Minnesota State Arts Board, through an appropria-
tion by the Minnesota State Legislature, and in part by a grant from the National
Endowment for the Arts. Significant support has also been provided by The
McKnight Foundation; Lannan Foundation; Jerome Foundation; Target Stores,
Dayton's, and Mervyn's by the Dayton Hudson Foundation; General Mills Foun-
dation; St. Paul Companies; Butler Family Foundation; Honeywell Foundation;
Star Tribune Foundation; James R. Thorpe Foundation; Bush Foundation;
The Lila Wallace Readers Digest Fund; James Lenfesty; the law firm of
Schwegman, Lundberg, Woessner & Kluth, P.A.; and many individual donors.
To you and our many readers across the country, we send our thanks for your
continuing support.

Coffee House Press books are available to the trade through our primary distribu-
tor, Consortium Book Sales & Distribution, 1045 Westgate Drive, Saint Paul, MN
55114. For personal orders, catalogs, or other information, write to: Coffee House
Press, 27 North Fourth Street, Suite 400, Minneapolis, MN 55401. Good books are
brewing at www.coffeehousepress.org.

LIBRARY OF CONGRESS CIP INFORMATION
Visit teepee town : native writings after the detours / edited by
    Diane Glancy and Mark Nowak.
        p.   cm.
      ISBN 1-56889-084-5 (pb : alk paper)
        1. American poetry—Indian authors. 2. Indians of North America—Poetry.
    3. American poetry—20th century. I. Glancy, Diane. II. Nowak, Mark.
    PS591.I55V57   1999
    811'.54080897—dc21   98-52208
                                                                    CIP

10   9   8   7   6   5   4   3   2   1

Contents

i–ii   PREFACE

iii–v   INTRODUCTION: *CRUIZING* THE ICEBERG

James Thomas Stevens / Aronhiòtas

1   *Tŏkinish*

Lise McCloud

20   Mixed American Pak

Gerald Vizenor

51   Excerpt from *Manifest Manners*

54   Museum Bound

56   Beaver

James Luna

68   Wet Dream Catcher

68   Hot Medicine Bag

69   You See What You Want

70   The Shameman

70   The Thinker

71   Guernica

Rosmarie Waldrop

72   from *A Key into the Language of America*
        Parts I, VI, VIII, XII, XIX, XXII, and XXIX

Marie Annharte Baker

82   One Appropriate First

84   'Rangutan Rage Writes About Story

85   Beware Writer

Carolyn Lei-lanilau

87 Hawaiians, no Kanaka, nah Hahh-Y-in

96 Ha'ina 'ia mai ana ka puana *(Let the Story Be Told)*

Barbara Tedlock

106 Pilgrimage

tj snow

118 Untitled

Linda Hogan

123 Germinal

124 What Has Happened to These Working Hands

125 Pillow

127 Elk Song

129 The History of Fire

130 Those Who Thunder

132 What Gets In

Wendy Rose

134 Subway Graffiti: An Anthropologist's Impressions

139 For the White Poets Who Would Be Indian

Maurice Kenny

140 Oroville High, California

141 Archeologist

142 Sweat

145 Reading Poems in Public

Hachivi Edgar Heap of Birds

147 Monetish
148 Want
149 Young Look
150 How Bout Them Cowboys
154 Ma-ka'ta l-na'-zin

Allison Adele Hedge Coke

155 The Change
161 Dog Road Woman
163 Wokiksuye
165 The Year of the Rat
185 Percheron Nambe Morning

Victoria Lena Manyarrows

188 The Language of Endangerment

Besmilr Brigham

190 To the Unwritten Poems of Young Joy
193 The Months Were Named For
194 the mask
195 Bread and Wine: The old Bread and Wine Mission
198 Heaved from Earth
200 The Arctic Thaw

Nora Marks Dauenhauer and Richard Dauenhauer

204 Yéil Yaagú/*Raven Boat*
210 The Woman Who Married the Bear

Diane Glancy

229 Tomatos

230 EEE AY WHO TWO

231 Death Cry for the Language

242 Mother of Mosquitos

Phil Young

251 Performance at Cherokee Trading Post (I-40, W. OK.)

252 Untitled (Red Man Chewing Tobacco)

253 I Cannot Speak (But I Can Write Jeep Cherokee)

254 Visit Teepee Town

Larry Evers and Felipe Molina

255 Coyotes in "Ringo Bwiapo":
On the Return of the Yaqui Song Tradition

Sherman Alexie

296 The Native American Broadcasting System

Juan Felipe Herrera

304 Nothing Is Taken That Is Not Given

Greg Sarris

310 The Verbal Art of Mabel McKay:
Talk as Culture Contact and Cultural Critique

Louise Bernice Halfe

332 Blue Marrow

Peter Blue Cloud

340   Coyote's Discourse on Power, Medicine,
and Would-be Shamans

347   Coyote's Anthro

351   Twenty Poet Sketches

361   CONTRIBUTORS

369   ACKNOWLEDGMENTS

preface

The nineteenth century was cataclysmic for Native American tribes. A way of life changed radically. What followed in the early twentieth century was a rumbling of silence and one or two voices that would become many by the end of the century. Voices explaining the meanings and possibilities of what Gerald Vizenor calls *Survivance.*

> There far off in the darkness, something happened. Far, far
> away in the nothingness, something happened. There was a
> voice, a sound, a word, and everything began.
>
> —N. Scott Momaday, *House Made of Dawn*

Native American writing began in flight, so to speak. In the nothingness of air. Then, somewhere, there was a voice. And another. Then other voices from lost cultures. This anthology is a collection of some of those voices built on an absence of place and identity. Voices built after the *detours* from the old ways of life.

Visit Teepee Town is a title which takes kitsch and the souvenir sound of *Indianness* and re-collects it in an act of stamping *original* back into the voice.

"Survival = Anger x Imagination," Sherman Alexie writes in *The Lone Ranger and Tonto Fistfight in Heaven.* Then comes Vizenor's *Survivance* which is survival with meaning. What takes the hollow space that anger leaves in these groups of writings? This collective Teepee Town. This new math. Imagination + Determination = Survivance.

There are new words, mixed languages, a redisposal of thought and feeling, and thought structures translated by the language that reconstructed them in the first place. The voice speaks new combinations of words and meanings and the co-beings that we are with them. After the detours, after the changes in directions.

Visit Teepee Town is an assemblage of words, a difference of tribes, different ways of explaining the new formats and finding new space.

—Diane Glancy

introduction

Cruizing the Iceberg

Once I saw a photo of an iceberg, the small of it above water, the mass below. It must have been taken from a submarine. Fightening to see how much was undercover. But for some reason, it is a reminder of the story of language. Written language with the oral tradition under it. The power of language in its speaking-into-being, the energy field that happens during *story*. It is the old power of oral tradition in that photo.

But we live in a written age. Orality turned into *writtality*, with its "task of learning how to hammer the voice onto page with those little nails called *alphabet*."[1] In other words, writing *kills* language. But under the writing, the old sound moves.

This collection of innovative North American Native writings peruses narratives which have been *iceberged* into dictionary meaning and proper usage. It looks at reverberations from the buried parts of language where vocables and the ghost of old languages are allowed (ALOUD) to echo in the forms and voices which explore contemporary and sometimes bilingual, sometimes visual, alternatives to stolid narrative. While predominantly a gathering of North American Native writers, this volume seeks to move beyond the purely assimilative and essentialist anthologies of the past, taking a more relationist stance by its inclusion of writers such as Chicano poet-theorist Juan Felipe Herrera's encounters with the Lacandón

Maya; German-American poet and translator Rosmarie Waldrop's work with both Narragansett language and Roger Williams's *A Key into the Language of America* (a book also explored by Mohawk poet James Thomas Stevens); University of Arizona Professor Larry Evers's collaboration with Felipe Molina on translations of Yaqui Coyote songs; and several other works.

This collection also foregrounds its resistance to, and provides evidence of, the Native survivance against academic social sciences as well as recent attempts to define contemporary/postmodern poetry & poetics which have either offered the erasure of North American Native authors or the overwriting of traditional Native American tales by ethnopoetic "total translations." These works represent a fraction of the recent postindian poetics exploring a revival of the magic of sound, the voice on which that sound rides, and the *un-nailing down of oral tradition.*

Actually, the intention of this collection of innovative native writings *cruizes* the persual. *Topographs* the text. Often in reading, words are intentionally misread and misplaced in order to fuzz, to blur, to unboundary. *Asyndetoning* the line of traffic. *Submarining* to get to what is beneath. Often these poems and poetic statements also formulate a reality that comes into being as the words are spoken; an atavism to the old belief that what was spoken actually came into being. These poems attempt to per(FORM), in their own way, a *ghost dance* in which the power of language to (FORM)ulate/re(FORM)ulate a lost or endangered world returns.

There's much going on in these writings. An iceberg made of water doesn't actually act like water. It acts more like land which it is not, but a third made of the one, not the two. But the third acting as if it were the second, the land. Well, try to bump into it as if it were not water, but water made tough as land to drive across, to *p'rooz.*

So what was once water now looks like something as though land, but still with the same element from which it was made. A different texture, shape, unbending, yet wistful as water and as dangerous, yet endangered itself if exposed to *warm*.

Read quicky, misread the possibilities of words and their happenings. At the same time, think of the *insertiveness* of these writings as a slow map of the poetics, the bricolages, the word possibilities *up-to-bat*. To ease past the significant detail and study of this field.

This perusal *cruize* through native writings. This *cruize* of *pair'roozing* the oral and written language.

Native thought expressed in English is something like a frozen territory. But in the variations of traffic, the old language is there almost before you know it, washing your windows. The gaudy, *goddy* iceberg tips. Just ask the Titanic who wins. It is the bifurcated, the one made of two with overlaps and *impages*.

Indian language often suffers from freezer burn. But call the frost away. Cross over the cold. *Car'ooz* the impound lot after snow. Rattle the thought of afterthought and underthought. Even the overthought. The new language recedes and mixes with the rubble of the old.

This collection focuses on voices which migrate as a language of endangerment (a term from the Vicky Manyarrows poem). It centers on a world both unretrievable and yet retrieving the impossibilities and invisibilities as written word is placed on the launching pad of its re(lease)ment.

—Diane Glancy and Mark Nowak

---

1 from "The Nail-down of Oral Tradition," *Claiming Breath,* Diane Glancy, University of Nebraska Press, 1992.

James Thomas Stevens/Aronhiòtas

Tōkinish

> **Tokinish** (tō kin ish) v. command meaning: "Wake him."
>> [Narragansett]

"Much comfort is not in much sleepe, when the most fearefull and most irrevocable Malediction is presented by thee, in a *perpetuall sleepe I will make their feasts, and I will make them drunke, and they shall sloope a perpetu all sleepe, and not wake.*"

—John Donne, *Devotions Upon Emergent Occasions*
from *Expostulation XV*

> "But yet the body is his booke."
>> —Donne

Awaunkeesitteoúwincohòck?	Who made you?
Wússuckwheke.	The book.

—Narragansett translation

To walk the periphery of islands, as if knowing the border of body.
To mould the well-muscled
                    curve of your back
modeled of river weeds hanging red on the scarp.
Water run down river rock,
the combe beneath your arm.
                Skin shining stone
                        as the sun settles into its own dumb ortho-
doxy.
Hemlock shoreline,
of trunks forced into silt's precision.

The vegetable earth on a mineral spine.

How to write island, the weighty peninsula of extremities.
The red of lichen on
a head of stone.

Weight is the catastrophe of what we don't know,
                    the unsleeping gravity drawing boat to shore.

❀

Acâwmuck notéshem.   I came over the water.
Mesh nomishoonhómmin.   I came by boat.
                    —Roger Williams, *A Key into the Language of America*

❀

Island.
Look to a map to prove the concept mute.
All waters have a source and this connection renders earth

island.

Is the naked-eye observance of a border
in every direction, the thing we call true?
Lack of continuity, the outline of matter.

❀

The island of a leaf in a yellow field of corn,
the island of a bowl, or objects on a table,
the island of a word.
I call your sleeping body island
because I know its white border.

❀

Roger Williams set foot in what would become Providence, Rhode
Island in 1636. Because he saw water on all sides he wrongly assumed
the land to be island. Although the Native he saw standing before him
was certainly isolated in isolated surroundings, he did not call him
island.

Tocketussawêitch?   What is your name?
Nníshishem.   I am alone.

❀

To say it requires a boat or bridge
to reach a true island
                          is to simplify the question too much.
A bridge or boat are simple movement.
When the boat is not moving across, it ceases to be boat
                          and a bridge is forever gerund.

Spanning implies movement, as when the bridge no longer spans the gap,
it ceases to be that bridge.

My hand as it reaches to touch your belly,
reaching to island or inland, the shallow dome
                                        and the mossy path
                        leading
                                to secret
                                        parts.

What remains secret in the two-fold nakedness
of the explorer,
                the naked find.

❁

  Paúskesu.   Naked.
  Pauskesítchick.   Naked men.
  Nippóskiss.   I am naked.

They have a two-fold nakednesse:

First ordinary and constant, when although they have a Beasts skin,
or an English mantle on, yet that covers ordinarily but their hinder parts
and all the foreparts from top to toe, (except their secret parts, covered with
a little Apron, after the patterne of their and our first Parents) I say all
else open and naked.

Their second nakednesse is when their men often abroad, and both men
and women within doores, leave off their beasts skins, or English cloth,
and so (excepting their little Apron) are wholly naked; . . .

—R.W.

❀

The earth with its skin of beasts,
a forested skin of leaf and bark,

        the live beast itself becoming skin.

The naked field opening fertile,

        and fertile forest woodland.

The jagged tops of trees mending
sky to earth,
the interlocking

        that for lack of, separates man from sky

                man from man.
Smooth skins that will not bind.

Clay to clay,
the coils of a vessel,

        require the scoring of a jagged stick.

A twisting trail to secret parts,
unclear,
most fertile, wild and overgrown. A river flows upward into sky.

❊

    Sepûo?   Is there a river?

    Toyusquanûo?   Is there a bridge?

Is there a bridge to that part of you, besides the one I call my own? If in definition, the bridge connects two isolated points, then we must decide when I reach to you, which body is isolated.

Or is isolation a mutual thing? If in its isolation, there is no recognition of its being "alone," no desire to become part to another, who rightfully calls it "island"?

❊

The Indians of Martins vineyard, at my late being amongst them, report generally, and confidently of some Ilands, which lie off from them to Sea, from whence every morning early, certaine Fowles come and light amongst them, and returne at Night to lodging, which Iland or Ilands are not yet discovered, though probably, by other Reasons they give, there is Land, &c.

                                          —R.W.

❊

Return at night to islands.
Fowl weaving into winds,
                    the wind woven into the quill itself.
A bird
navigating the water's edge, searching the familiar
a vineyard of grapes,
                    can remind you of a thing you knew on the body.
A thing perhaps you tasted once
                    and through its naming became owner.
This is the benefit of exploration.

❀

Wattàp.   A root of Tree.
Wómpimineash.   Chesnutts.
Wuttáhimneash.   Strawberries.
Peshaùiuash.   Violet leaves.
Wenómeneash.   Grapes.

Corralation of recognized sense, mapping the body in response to
memory and stimuli. The texture of your open eye across my tongue
like a new grape with its skin peeled back.

Asqútasquash, *their Vine aples, which the* English *from them call*
Squashes *about the bignesse of Apples of severall colours, a sweetness. . . .*
                                                    —R.W.

❀

It can remind you of a thing you knew on the body,

what you called it in your search for the familiar.
                           Did it relate to a stone, an apple, or element?
The basic paradox of language,
that its inconsistencies should make it most useful.

"I cannot heare of any disease of the stone amongst them."

When there is nothing more disparate
than stone from disease,
the apple from Adam, sin from knowledge.

Walk the islands above a waterfall

                              pressing your heels into the silt.

Call this imprint: *Qunnamaŭgsuck*—the first that come in the
Spring into the fresh Rivers.

This might mean Lamprey
and there is a consequence.

❀

I have learned to say each word with caution,
                              your body or any body,
I will not call *mine*.

    Wuhóck.   The body.
    Nohòck: cohòck.   My body, your body

The first to come
found baskets of corn

          and brought them away without payment.
To know the feel and taste of a thing

          as if knowing implies its ownership.

When if both employ the same word,   *mine,*

    familiarity with language blinds the user to contradiction,
    action leads to reaction and consequence.

The next were met and assailed with arrows.

             ❀

The arrow might remind you of birds

        and no one can say you are wrong.
The feathered fletching
and obsidian beak.

The history of the word is inseparable from the word
though susceptible to change.

As Augustine:

"Words were not adopted by men because they have intrinsic
meaning, rather they have a meaning because men have agreed
upon them."

             ❀

The arrowroot plant
discovered in the *New* World
                  was called by the Arawak people: aru-aru
meaning "meal of meals."

The process of the unfamiliar changed to familiar.
Folk etymology refashions the *aru-aru* to *arrowroot,*
                denies a word of its infinite history.

The shape of a word
cannot save itself from its symbol,
              that is a pointed leaf
                  or a nectar drawing poison.

Your *demeanor* as *mirror,*
vain thought that conscience
           denies to speech.

❁

As history changes, we create the history of change.
There is loss,
like a building that rebuilds its facade with the age,
to please the ageless.
Growth is replaced by vanity, if vanity is owning.

❁

The deeds of transfer of their lands by the Indians in Rhode Island
are recorded, with the signatures of the sachems appended in the form of
their attested marks of a bow, an arrow, tomahawks and other devices,
significant of a sign manual.

—Winslow, *Chronicles of the Pilgrims*

❀

To create sign manuals for a life
is a reductive task.
                They would call it totemic,
a history of emotion and actions, consumed by the sign of a hatchet.
Considering what distinguishes the language of symbol from the
language of mineral fact,

≈ ☉ ≈   this could mean island or the man who lives alone.

Deeds become obscure. Possession is transient.

❀

What if no translation exists for the sign?

A bow exists for the English as the shape of the bow itself.
The Narragansett know the bow as *Onúttug:* A halfe Moone in war.

I know you as *Pleasure* and the symbol of its origin,
that is not a collective sign.

❀

To affix one's name to a thing
a name which is symbol for a life, which acts as the sign of possession
in conjunction with the thing.

"The Indians of Martins vineyard, at my late being amongst them, . . ."

Martin becomes victim to word phenomenon
as *Martha's* Vineyard sees the map,

consider the *aru-aru* . . .

❀

Beneath your white forearm,
the network of vein.
Unfamiliar, you say *bloodpath*
and I hear *blueprint*,
because it suits my cause.
To understand
your arm as bridge, the impossible engineering
written beneath
your skin.

❀

Island in islands.
Cells course the channels
                    of a living country,
thick with voyage
                    and the shipwreck of intercourse.
Identical islands
on the span of your chest
                    ringed with riverweed,
red as rock.

"Such sinews even in thy milk, and such things in thy words, . . ."
                                        —Donne

❀

Sinews of the bowstrand,
from the beast itself comes its end.

Its skin retaining the dimensions of the body
and the signature of every wound.

The scar on your inner thigh
is landmark
                    and I might think I've found my way,
call to you.

❀

The way a bird cries out
to travel

      beyond the perimeters of its body.

A note from the sycamore belongs to the field.

What is the open window but an extension of home.

         ❀

The field as garment,
echoes reclaiming,

      physical shifts below.

    Mauúnshesh.   Goe slowly or gently.
    Taguatchòwash.   Goe up hill.

Rows of corn
in incessant precision
mould the furrows, at the forehead of every work.
At night to turn and return,
I mould the curve of your back.

Garment gone and naked to the sky,
to the earth spinning gravity,

      your limbs in close around me.

         ❀

The field and its touch,
familiar surround you,

          the smell of warm straws
and a light summer mold.

Then comfort comes in recognition.

✿

In the billowing of thunderheads
to recognize a hare, a face or an event,
delights the viewer through familiarity.

Of taste or touch,
the fields are flickering with the knowledge of likeness.

The taste of salt
on the inside of your arm
calls to voyage.
The shimmering bow as the ship comes in.

✿

The thrill of recognition.

What cheare Nétop? *is the generall salutation of all*
English toward them. Nétop *is friend.*

Netompaûog.   Friends.

They are exceedingly delighted with Salutations in their own Language.
—R.W.

❀

Every translator has to be two people,
an Indian
            assigned a mark on paper.

A berry-stained moon on a birch palimpsest.

How to paint the name of the moon, which is *Munnánnock*
or the moon itself which is *Nanepaùshat.*

❀

The hemlock on the shoreline
gives up its flat needles
to a vertical line
                    topped by a sphere.

Line river on a map
and the loss of its scent,
the gravel sound of suckling
after a surge.

                    ❀

To make maps of a lover's body is
the sad border of a shoulder
                    playing harbour to the head,
not to be reconciled
                    by a thin black line.
Or even the broken line
that allows the shifting border,
the dumb index
                    that lacks reflection on the eye.
The compass rose
has lost its magnet
where north is not north
                    but the head on its side.

                    ❖

There is a space between your torso and mine, where travel goes. The charting of my course is instinctual but I give destination no name, as the name for you lacks more than its symbol. You are an island or the name of an island. A name is a bony skeleton, with angles protruding. A ruinous anatomy like the word for swamp, mountain or fish, awaiting the mind to return its mineral matter. Your body doesn't wait for a name, because it has one in the circumference of my arms, where only the skin can speak it.

❀

To steady the body in human intellection,
I relate your parts to home.
Lying in fold, beside this sleeping island,

the nurturing native of your skin,
ribbed rack of meats and warmth from the night

> *In him I have found a House, a Bed,*
> *A Table, Company . . .*

❀

Remembering just how the light stood
on the water surrounding home,

I cannot make love to the same body twice
where the flow of emotion is constant.

Cells charged with melancholy
now vibrate with pleasure.

VISIT TEEPEE TOWN

Sepûo?	Is there a River?
Mishquínash.	The vaines.

※

Néepuck.	The blood.
Wunnícheke.	The hand.
Wunnáks.	The bellie.
Mapànnog.	The breast.
Apòme.	The thigh.
Sítchipuck.	The necke.
Wuttòne.	The mouth.
Wuskeésuckquash.	The eyes.
Mscáttuck.	The fore-head.

The tension surrounding your eyes at the moment life comes to a
head. Nothing planted or harvested but the winnowing of a day's
events. Bark to basket, gathering parts. Island among islands, archi-
pelago.

". . . such voyages, such peregrinations to fetch remote and
precious metaphors, such extensions, such spreadings,
such curtains of allegories, . . ."

—Donne

※

Allegory of conquest, the shipwreck of intercourse.
Alone, the bloody tenant is left to translate history without voice,
a language inherent.

Native Writings After the Detours

Lise McCloud

Mixed American Pak:
NATIONAL HOLIDAY THUNDER CHRYSANTHEMUM
WITH PEARLS & REPORTS

✱✱✱✱✱Bang ✱✱✱✱✱Bang ✱✱✱✱✱ POP ✱ POP ✱ POP
✱✱✱✱✱ Bang ✱✱✱✱✱

Working at the plastic factory, working in the mental home, working at a desk job, working, working, working all the holidays but one. Years of scrips & scrapts in U-HAUL boxes acting as my furniture—

O boy! O joy! It is Independence Day in the land of the free. This will be a documentary labeled *A Pearl of Time,* a string of things, a mixed memoir with a roadside fireworks stand and a cornfield and a corny joke, corny laugh, straw hat on a sunburned woman holding up for the camera a NEWS TRANSMITTER D.O.T. Class C Consumer Explosive.

❁

Fishing Report: Roaming down old highway 81, the ancient glacial seashore. White Rock Dam, South Dakota, 7/4/94: Smoked salmon, fried chicken, deviled eggs, ham & Swiss & Dijon sandwiches, baked

beans, roasted wieners, garden salad, fluffy biscuits with sweet cream
butter & homemade chokecherry jelly & raspberry & wild plum jam
& sunflower honey, assorted cheese, crackers, Doritos, marinated arti-
choke hearts, grandma's giant made-from-scratch decorated with little
odds & ends cupcakes in a star-spangled-night enamel roaster, cold
watermelon too, red white & blue star-sprinkled chocolate cake
with cumulonimbus frosting and whirligig vortex of sharply cloven
Snickers bar triangles on top. The fishing is no good today, who cares.

❀

The pearl of the prairie, the legend we seek, is the sacred White
Rock. Therefore our afternoon excursion takes us down the slope of
the ancient glacial shoreline and across the phantom seabed, a vast
mud plain eerily scattered with rocks, boulders, skeletons (the bones
of farm machines and farmsteads and an elm picked white and clean).
Flocks of terns and gulls skim the phantom tide. We are submerged
in the inexplicable tide of Lake Agassiz, pulled toward the ghost
town. The ghost town is visible as a distant green raft of trees which
we approach singing stupidly. Vocalizing, rather, a version of "Name
That Tune" in which the only musical clues are absurd wordless
noises related to the theme: Ghost Riders in the Sky, The Ghost
of a Chance, The Ghost of Route 109, etc. (the dead tree smooth
and barkless with its arms still raised in supplication) (an *act of God*
is lightning). The theme tunes from "Ghostbusters" "Casper the
Friendly Ghost" "Phantom of the Opera," and so on (or perhaps an
act of certain beetles is what the tree succumbed to, a fine example
of *denuded)* (a word casting the deceased in a different light now,
a bare-naked dance for nobody living in this noplace).
A song dog waits in nearby hiding for the moon.

South Dakota is the Coyote State, North Dakota is the Flickertail State, Minnesotans refer to even a very specific place in either state as being "in the Dakotas." The flickertails stand bolt upright at comically nervous attention along the road to White Rock, SD, POP. 2 as we approach the pockmarked sign. Hail and bullets always find these forlorn markers. The town is reportedly named for a large white boulder around which it once prospered.

There is always one flickertail who will break under the strain and hurl itself suicidally under your vehicle and escape miraculously unharmed just as you're trying to pass it. I have seen a flickertail scrambling madly about under a speeding vehicle ahead of me on the highway, having made the dash in a frenzy of indecision. Usually they just stand about trying to get a better view and neurotically jerking their tails. People from other parts of the country don't notice our small rodent mascot unless it's pointed out, and then they tend to believe that it's a prairie dog.

We motor slowly through the streets of White Rock, looking for signs of its two living citizens: A glassed box nailed to a corner pole, displaying a fake red rose and minutes of the most recent town meeting (Paid the power company, $68.69. Paid the telephone company, $42.71). Neatly mowed roadsides with intervals of wild asparagus carefully missed by the mower. A well-kept white frame church with red roof. A couple of elderly houses in good repair with trim lawns and paint jobs, many perky hobby-shop birdhouses (a cunning wren cabin, an apartment complex for purple martins, a wood duck house, a cottage for finches in the empty lots turning to forest where people once lived). Deer glide from the yards of the battered and sagging grey stick houses, vanish into the tangled growth of box elder with just one haunting glance back. A sleek 1930s robin's-egg blue phaeton keeps slipping around the corners ahead of us before we can even get a look at the ghost who's driving it. The little boys are more impressed with this phenomenon than with the ectoplasm we found dumped by the crossroad. They haven't been around long enough to notice the regional pattern of 4th of July antique car shows.

Two giant cottonwoods and a slab of sparkly red granite tell us we are in the business district. There is nothing visible but an apparent sculpture of a giant Idaho baking potato made of welded spray-painted white reinforcing rods. The granite marker communicates that in its heyday, pioneer White Rock boasted banks, hotels, mercantile and grocery stores, restaurants, blacksmith shops, grain mills, saloons, dance halls and even an opera house. The town was quickly outgrowing its original plat, where it wanted a grain elevator erected, but this big white rock was in the way. Skyscraper of the prairie, highly visible symbolic manifestation of progress—the grain elevator was a new important landmark. Now I see what happened. White people never did believe what lives in such a rock. So they got a load of dynamite, and they blew the rock to smithereens, and unhoused its displeased ghost. A series of civic misfortunes followed. Only the skeletal re-bar monument is left to represent old White Rock. Only the venerable cottonwoods lived to whisper this glum tale.

❁

BOOM!

❁

7/4/96: I always like to observe the 4th of July. I live in the Sunset Trailer Court, have two pink plastic flamingos and a plastic birdbath in my yard, three kids who are pretty sure they saw the featured suspect on *America's Most Wanted* or *Unsolved Mysteries* just a few trailers down or in the Stop-N-Go. Sunset Court used to be a field of sunflowers and corn and sometimes soybeans way north of town, just north of the north 40 of the Bureau of Indian Affairs boarding school where I was growing up. The Chicago & Western track ran past these fields then the Wahpeton Indian School then the town and rickety old Peavey grain elevators right after that. In the spring-time, wild prairie roses bloomed along the track so exactly like luminous pink Ojibway floral beadwork it makes me wish them back, right now. There. They smell pure, like a blessing. Like rain. One drop held in a petal, *glistering* in the sun. Anyone impatient enough to go AWOL in the daylight could follow the tracks this far out and see that there was suddenly nothing else to see but rows of green things zooming into and colliding in infinity, the horizon I saw then as yet unobstructed.

❀

TOP TEN FIREWORKS I WOULD WANT TO SEE IN BEADWORK:
1. OPENING FLOWER WITH HAPPY BIRD
2. PLUM FLOWERS REPORT SPRING
3. 96 COLOUR PEARL FLOWERS WITH REPORT
4. WEEPING DAFFODILS
5. MAMMOTH CHRYSANTHEMUM
6. SILVER CHRYSANTHEMUM ZENITH
7. NO. 300 3 COLOR-CHANGING CHRYSANTHEMUM
8. SUNFLOWER SPINNER
9. CRACKLING CARNATION WITH BLUE
10. SWORD ORCHID FOUNTAIN

❀

Perhaps the most daring and determined AWOL in memory was the boy counted absent just before a long school bus trip in the 1960s. Police were notified, the town was combed, but the mass bus trips had to go on as scheduled. It was the start of summer vacation when all the students, maybe four hundred in number, were being taken back to their home reservations in the Dakotas, Montana, Wyoming, Nebraska, Minnesota, Wisconsin, and a few other far-flung places. My father and other teachers were driving the buses, as they always did; in those days there were only about forty staff to the whole operation. Sometimes I rode along, since it was the only chance I'd get to see the world and travel. The northbound buses were to stop near the little town of Hillsboro, about ninety miles up the highway, and meet at the wayside rest for a picnic. When the second bus pulled in and parked in the shade, people from the first bus noticed something fall out from under it. When they went over to investigate they found the missing boy, who had been clinging to the undercarriage all the way from Wahpeton. He was lying on the ground, in a state of complete, dazed, and speechless exhaustion, but otherwise unharmed.

❁

TIGERS ROARING FOUNTAIN, SNOW AND RED PLUM ROCKET, DRAGON DANCING WITH PHOENIX, OVERLORD IN THE SKIES, JUMBO GLITTEROUS LIGHT ROCKET, NO. 300 GALAXY OF STROBING STARS, WARMING GREETING (61 SHOTS PEARLS & REPORTS)

⽕

Wahpeton is an old tribal meeting ground at the confluence of three rivers. The Red River of the North is formed by the Ottertail River, which has its source in the eastern forest and lake country, and the Bois de Sioux which proceeds up from Lake Traverse between Minnesota and South Dakota. The Red River Valley is a strip of land thirty to ninety miles wide running north-south and is the bottom of the glacial Lake Agassiz which was seven hundred miles long. Wave action of the receding lake caused different beaches that one can notice while traveling across the Valley. I was born just a few hundred yards from the headwaters of the Red, on the Minnesota bank as there was no hospital in Wahpeton. The Red River flows north into Lake Winnipeg in Canada which is a remnant of the huge inland sea.

Turtle Mountain Chippewa and Devils Lake Sioux runaways ran north all night on the tracks, to the grain elevator at Brushvale, Minnesota, and hid inside till someone caught up with them and took them back to Wahpeton. The other Sioux sometimes hopped a Chicago & Western boxcar down to South Dakota. The tracks are gone now, along with the rural era that they symbolized. Gone is the little lone grove of native trees on the western skyline, where townsfolk used to go and poke around for arrowheads in the ruins of long-dead campfires. In 1971 the new highway bypass cut down and ran over that solitary marker. The usual suburban, industrial sprawl ensued. It's not to wax nostalgic by attempting to fix in place, to reconstruct, remember. By the age of ten I understood that there was never going to be anything for me in Wahpeton. I would have to run off to the mountains and live inside a tree like this boy in a movie I had seen, or build a raft and float away on the Red, or steal a horse from the barnyard by the tracks with the wild plum and Russian olive trees running alongside it that's now the trailer court section. I packed up a hobo bundle many times for practice, made lists. At some point in history the local fireworks stand brought a nagging mysterious whisper of the Orient into my small, dull, homogenous corner of the USA. I picked up and pieced together the tissue paper that someone ripped off a package. And understood that it was a deviant trait to notice the exotic Chinese written characters and illustrations and oddly behaved English of the product wrappers—to wonder at these frail missives from the oppressed but poetry-minded commies on the far side of the planet.

❀

BLUE PALM, SPARKLING TREEFIREWORKS, NO. 300 PLUM TREE, NO. 200 RAIN WILLOW, NOISY FOUNTAIN

❀

In 1904 a resident of the city, Senator Porter J. McCumber, introduced a bill "to establish an Indian agricultural college at or near the city of Wahpeton, in the county of Richland." This was the same person responsible for the McCumber Agreement or "Ten-Cent Treaty" of 1892, whereby the Turtle Mountain band of Chippewa Indians were forced to cede ten million acres of the richest land on the continent for the perverse sum of ten cents per acre. In 1904 the school was created by an act of Congress, the McCumber agreement was ratified, and the disastrous government Indian policies of the Allotment Era found their perfect vehicle at Wahpeton.

The first crowd brought to this pseudomilitary outpost were the dispossessed children of Turtle Mountain. My grandpa graduated from Wahpeton Indian School in 1923. He started in 1912 at the age of seven, with time at Flandreau Indian School in South Dakota and Haskell Institute in Kansas. You could enter first grade here and never leave until it was time to go down to Flandreau, then Haskell, then the great mythic melting pot. An early-1900s photo captioned "United States Indian School" shows a line of stark brick buildings on a treeless grid of dirt with tufts of native grasses still hanging on the fringes. Immense, dark, and strictly foreboding, these were the very same structures which occupied my early view of the world; their demolition in the 1960s seemed like a WWII movie or similar apocalypse simply because they were the community I knew up to then. The bricks were of a peculiar deep ferrous shade like drying blood, and I have never since seen their type anywhere. They were heavy, inhabited bricks, dense with the forces of human and geo-logic history that had pressed them into the U.S. Indian Service. And they were speckled through with tiny, tiny little lovely sea-shells! If you hoped to pry a wee white ocean clamshell out of a brick in the wall and keep it for a treasure, it would break and leave a scar like smallpox. These walls housed a vast unseen ghost made of unresolved grief, violent wind, and black shadows, but every sum-mer they upheld the swaying silk gowns, the unspeakable swooning beauty of the federal-Indian hollyhocks.

❁

VIOLETS & CRIMSONS, DANCING FRESH FLOWERS, BEAUTIFUL BUDS, GROUND-BLOOMING FLOWERS, ATTRACTIVE FLOWERS, COLOR PEARL FLOWERS, GREEN GLITTEROUS FLOWERS, FLORAL SHELL

❁

My older sister and her glam girlfriends of the secret exclusive Tibby Club and her showbiz *wintke* friend held hollyhock doll beauty pageants and Cinderella balls. You take a full blossom—

the pale buttery yellow, or the rich rich magenta, or the virginal
white, or the fairy pink, or the voluptuous purple—and poke a
toothpick through the center. Then you put a medium size green
bud on for the bosom and poke a toothpick crossways for arms
and put a little head bud on the top of this. Try to find a bud with
a little flare of color bursting out, like a hairdo.

❀

GOLDEN FLOWER FOUNTAIN, GREEN GLITTERING FLOWER
TRI-COLOR SPRAYER, HAPPY SILVER FLOWERS, PEACH FLOWERS,
TRI-ANGLE WHISTLING FLOWERS, GOLDEN SILVER-FLOWERS,
MAMMOTH PEONY

❀

This is not "a longing for experiences, things, or acquaintanceships
belonging to the past." This is a salvage operation. A dive into the
wreck even knowing that this life is sink or swim against the cur-
rent. I am a minor and contrary organism, swimming the invisible
tides of the ghost lake.

❀

After the buffalo were gone, my great-grandfather contracted to
gather their bones across the plains and haul them to some location
on the railroad, maybe Minot. His previous occupation had of course
been a buffalo hunter. The bones were piled up in mountains along-
side the tracks, shipped in boxcars to cities like Detroit for industrial
purposes like being crushed into fertilizer. But my great-grand-
mother took a pair of buffalo horns and carefully polished them

Native Writings After the Detours

with boot black and wrapped the bone bridge in a precious scrap of black velvet and beaded it with flowers.

They were reservation Indians in 1892, not long married, setting out to make their living by farming the unfarmable land of the reservation as in the McCumber Agreement. They raised grain and vegetables and a pig or two, kept a cow and sometimes chickens. Even deer had become rare, but they say that before the sun was up great-grandma traversed the woods and the hills hunting squirrels, birds, rabbits. She rigged up some kind of trap involving a door and a bed-spring, which suddenly dispatched unsuspecting crowds of birds that came for the grain she had sprinkled outside the family cabin. Although great-grandpa was angered to see the beautiful songbirds fall victim to this particular enterprise, it kept a dozen kids fed and busy on a cold day in winter. Great-grandma could make a few coins at different times of the year by selling butter and cream to the trader, selling wild reservation berries to the farmers' wives down on the prairie, selling cranberry bark and a certain medicinal root to the pharmaceutical company buyer (these ended up in patent medicines such as the one labeled as Lydia Pinkham's Vegetable Compound). Great-grandma would sometimes drive her horse and buggy down from Turtle Mountain, sixty miles down the road to the pioneer town of Rugby, at the geographic center of North America where the handsome wooden train depot yet stands. There she sold her beadwork to tourists for a price I do not know. If these heirlooms were valued at all by passing strangers, they perhaps are preserved in some far-off museum. They were the nearest thing to family jewels an Indian woman had, but they did not get handed down among family members. I do have a small circular drawstring coin purse that my great-grandmother gave to my grandmother who gave it to my mother who gave it to me.

It is a purse of many colors. It is a thing that saw good use.
I know this because it is an object made of leftovers, of irregular
beads sewed concentrically on soft, worn doeskin, and not a long
painstaking work of art that someone would have purchased. I can
see the different kinds of beads that my great-grandmother used
to create her vanished treasure, a sampler of antique beads all at
hand in this circle. I can see her put a few silver coins into it and
walk away from the train depot without the flowering art she spent
so many patient hours at, sorting every bead to the right size and
shape and shade and prayerful result that she surely would have
rather left behind her, a half century later, in her Turtle Mountain
home.

One day in the 1950s or 60s Relocation era of federal-Indian
history my uncle happened to be walking down an alley in Grand
Forks, North Dakota, where he was trying to work or go to college
or be otherwise assimilated into non Indian society. There he saw
some people packing up and moving out of their large fine house.
Heaped by the alley were all manner of items to be discarded.
Decades after he first laid eyes on it, he recognized his grand-
mother's beaded bison horn memorial perched atop the rubbish pile.
He retrieved it, and despite a bumpy life of relocation, has kept it in
a safe and honored place all these years.

❁

GARDEN-INSPIRING FIREWORKS, BLOSSOMING GARDEN,
GUEST GREETING GARDEN

❁

July 4, 1994. Raining fast and steady all morning, nothing to see on TV but *Anne of the Thousand Days* with Geneviève Bujold as Anne Boleyn, Richard Burton as Henry VIII. The boys are restless, impatient for everything to dry up so they can see fireworks. "What is the Fourth of July for?" "So there will be no more kings in this land." The radio reports a high chance of continued bad weather, a "trailer court shooting" in Minnesota. Sky stops pouring, sun comes out, we pack up and spend the day in South Dakota, sight a small funnel cloud on the way home. At 9:38 P.M., people accumulate in Chahinkapa Park waiting for the town fireworks show to officially be canceled. Trucks and vans with Texas plates have the picnic parking spots already. Barbecue smoke rises up slowly into the drizzle, falls down all around with a tantalizing sizzle. The migrant workers are setting off rockets, cones, Roman candles, dancing over exploding chains of firecrackers. Big boys on bikes ride by: "He's gonna blow up his cojones." "Cooking prairie oysters, ha ha."

❁

Old Wild Rice was my many-times-great grandfather and the first documented ancestor to migrate into the Red River country and work in the furbiz industry. So it has been since the late 1700s that this writer's history has its source in the Valley. The ancestor was born on an island in Lake Superior and led a canoe brigade out of the woodlands to begin a Plains culture transition. My grandpa named him as Gaytay Mahnomin, meaning Old Wild Rice, from the handed-down tales; he was a considerable personage still spoken of in the 1900s. The traders Henry and Chaboillez, in their 1797 – 1801 fur trade journals, referred to him variously as The Great Chief Manomine, Old Menominee, Vieux Folle Avoine, Old Fallewine,

Crazy Oats and Old Wild Oats, probably signifying his origins in the wild rice country, but just as aptly tweaking a tribal progenitor.

To make a long story short, the furbiz men married the Indian women and started a mixedblood, furtrade society whose modern incarnation after the passing of the mixedblood, bison-based society and subsequent reservation poverty was the Bureau of Indian Affairs and Indian Health Service cultures, two massive federal-Indian vertical hierarchies where persons with sufficient skills and blood quantum to meet the paperwork requirements could find a niche or a college education. Education being an historical treaty provision, I would be happy to go along collecting degrees as long as the grass shall grow and the rivers shall flow, but everybody needs $, have worked in BIA, IHS with the same Indian and fur trade surnames as in the historical treaty and trade journal documents. My brothers, sisters, and I grew up in a federal-Indian enclave by Dad's tour of duty at Turtle Mountain agency in the 1950s then transfer down to Wahpeton. A full-blooded German from Minnesota, he was lured by somewhat exaggerated reports of skiing opportunities at Turtle Mountain.

❁

In October of 1992, I step outside a seedy bat-infested apartment in Minnesota, where I have gone to obtain a graduate degree in something of supposed use to the national Indian health problem. I open my mailbox as a foolish hopeful ritual, because a few years earlier on the Turtle Mountain reservation I learned that one can sometimes get a check this way or at least a blink of motivation. (I have *never* got a *cruel* rejection note from anywhere, but literary acceptances with payment are just about as rare.) There's a discount outlet where you can get ten loaves of not quite moldy bread for a dollar on

Tuesdays and that's where I'm headed, because you can fuel, or fool, a family of boys *indefinitely* on grilled commodity cheese sandwiches and date-expired Ho-Hos. To my total shock, there is a check from the U.S. Treasury in San Francisco, made out to me in the amount of $1,729.76. It is "La Pay" from the Ten-Cent Treaty that everyone was waiting for all this time and meanwhile died of old age and hardship. In a daze I call up different meat lockers and finally order half a beef to be delivered. Nobody had any bison.

❖

Good Sport Report: My younger sister H and her husband J come down July 3rd, 1994 meaning to escape the heat and din of the Cities. J is forced to rescue a man from a burning house they notice on the way out. The guy is on the phone, miffed with J's persistent interruption, doesn't want to hang up and acknowledge the inferno. Finally the guy is dragged out, fire engines hose down the house, H and J continue on to Wahpeton and knock on the door. "Mom, my godmother, godfather, and god-dog are here." They have a rehabilitated greyhound they adopted from the racetrack. Even after his near immolation, J is running every which way for hours, performing safety maneuvers and pyrotechnic feats ("close adult supervision"). The things that we thought were harmless bottle rockets turn out to be flesh-seeking FESTERING SCUDS. Although we follow all the correct steps to point them at nowhere they only want to go in people's windows or on the heads of those getting out of a car in a parking lot a block down the street. One of them starts the entrance to the apartment building across the street on fire, J runs over and using his big feet and a rug deftly stamps and smothers it out, "I've had practice." The videotape of all this looks quite a bit like the Desert Storm news recording from 1991 when I dig them both out of a U-HAUL box the next winter.

Consumer Report: After the A.M. rain, a last-minute investigation of area fireworks stands turns up a MIXED AMERICAN economy pak assortment and a 2-for-1 sale on the item labeled SMALL BFFS. The small bffs sound like a dud, an ineffectual trifle that might produce a minor spark and puff of smoke then go spluttering into the wet grass to die. Just the thing for three small boys too hell-bent on acquiring artillery skills. After midnight, all the goods with exciting names like SONIC JACK, THOR MISSILE, SATURN MISSILE BATTERY, BANSHEE WHISTLING AIR BOMB ROCKET, AMERICAN DOGFIGHT, AERIAL CROSSFIRE, 61-SHOTS NATIONAL HOLIDAY, MAXIMUM LOAD lie in acrid tatters on the lawn. Time for the small bffs, a suitable anticlimax to the day's war, get them all lit and done with. "Yikes!" "Holy Shit!" Uncle John is in the crossfire. They're all over us like hornets. That is when I realize that the Chinese writer left two vital strokes out, and small bffs belong in the pyrotechnic family that includes KILLER BEES, CRAZY BEES, DEVIL CLUSTER BEEHIVE.

Whizzzzz   !!!   Bang

❋ ❋ ❋

FAVORITE INSECT-INSPIRED FIREWORKS
WITH RUNNER-UP ARACHNID:

1.   SMALL BEES
2.   CRAZY BEES (/ TUBES WITH PEARLS & REPORTS)
3.   CLUSTERING BEES
4.   KILLER BEES
5.   HAPPY BEES

6. YELLOW BEES

7. JUMBO BEES ROCKET

8. BEES & FLOWERS

9. GLISTERING BUTTERFLIES

10. DANCING BUTTERFLIES

11. CLUSTERING CICADAS
    (61 SHOTS WHISPERING COLOURED BOUQUET)

12. RISING WHISTLE CICADA

13. PRAISE GOOD CICADA

14. GLORIOUS CRICKETS

15. NO. 200 GOLDEN SPIDER

❁

Mixed American Report: From time to time at Turtle Mountain, elders mentioned to me their school experiences with a hint— sometimes subtle, sometimes not—that a Turtle Mountain mixed-blood did not enjoy the highest niche of prestige in the boarding school system. This could not have been strictly a matter of genetics. Most if not all students would have been "mixed" to some degree or another by the early 1900s, and a Turtle Mountain "Michif" might be more Indian than the perceived "fullbloods." No, it was the perennial problem of everybody trying, without sufficient social or historical perspective or an informed frame of reference, to categorize the Michif. If you wished to give one of them an English translation for their Indian name, they already had a French one. They were called a band of Chippewa, but were a Plains buffalo culture. They loved to dance, but were likely to require a fiddle instead of a drum, performing a crazy blur of bagpipe and Indian steps known as the Red River Jig. They were uncanny linguists.

If you taught them a noun in English they would attach a French
article and gender to it, as well as a Plains-Cree verb phrase, and
maybe even a Hudson's Bay Company burr if the noun had an R
sound (nonexistent in the Algonquian tongues). As Plains Indians
the Turtle Mountain Chippewa were not even famous for any
battles or massacres involving the u.s. Army (who were latecomers
on the scene, this bunch having already figured out centuries earlier
how to get along with non-Indians). In innumerable other ways
the Turtle Mountain Chippewa refused to behave as an acceptable
stereotype, and instead were a truly disappointing, exasperating,
adapting variety of native!

"You are not really Indians but a poor class of French," a teacher
at Bismarck Indian School told a girl from Turtle Mountain, whose
voice sixty years later conveyed the sting of that remark. Another
girl, arriving at the Wahpeton Indian School and starting the first
day of classroom instruction in her life, experienced a feeling of
deep inferiority and embarrassment when the children were asked
to announce their names for the teacher. One by one, the children
of the plains, mountain, and woodland tribes told the teacher their
names. American Horse, Black Thunder, Chasing Hawk . . . "Oh!
Wonderful! How beautiful!" the teacher exclaimed and printed and
wrote in her exquisite Palmer cursive on her blackboard the names,
so that everyone could see how beautiful and wonderful they
looked. Running Deer, Spotted Eagle, Yellow Bird . . . the Turtle
Mountain girl was gripped with dread as her turn approached,
wishing she could tell the teacher anything but *Parisien*. . . . Coming
from the train depot, she had already seen many marvelous and
unfamiliar new sights of civilization and learned the names for
them. There was even a big grand cake of a house with a fence of
pointed iron spears all around it (possibly Senator McCumber's

house, by the description) and in the yard was caged the most astonishing, gorgeous creature in all the world. "And what is your name?" the teacher asked her. The little Michif girl leapt beamingly to her feet. "My name is *Parrot*," she proudly pronounced to her audience.

❀

AWK!

❀

TEN FAVORITE ORNITHOLOGICAL DISTRACTIONS &
2-WAY ALTERNATIVE

1. 61-SHOTS SILVERY EAGLE BALL
2. WILD GEESE ROCKET WHISTLING
    WITH RED & GREEN FLOWERS
3. MANDARIN DUCK DISPORTING WATER
4. CHIRPING ORIOLE
6. FRIGHTENED BIRDS
7. HUNDRED BIRDS
8. HEN LAYING EGGS
9. COCK CROWING AT DAWN
10. JR. CUCKOO
11. CUCKOO CUCKOO

❀

A Pearl: Rummaging in the fireworks displays, I come across an item labeled simply HAPPY.

A Pearl: Rummaging in a box of old papers, I come across a group
of reports written by Indian students in the 1920s. The teacher had
evidently encouraged the pupils to capture on paper their oral tradi-
tions. Some were trickster tales and creation legends, but the boy
with the French last name had something resembling a European
fairy tale featuring an Indian princess and the winning of her hand
by the most unlikely in her Chief father's eyes suitor with the help
of the boy's magic horse, "and he was sparkling her," said the loop-
de-loop, skipping, leaping, dot the i cross the t dance of the child's
newly-acquired fountain pen cursive, and I remember the imaginary
writing that children do as they run along in the summer night with
their briefly blazing wand of spitting stars.

GLORY TORCH SPARKLER, SUPER CHARGED FLASHLIGHT FIRECRACK-
ERS BOMB, WHISTLING MOON TRAVELERS WITH REPORT, THUNDER
BOMBS, BLACK CAT BOTTLEROCKET, TURTLE, FROG, BLOWFISH,
MONKEY DRIVE, MONKEY DANCING & 12 SPINNING JACKS

A Pearl: Checking out another fireworks display, I come across a
thing called DAKOTA DAZZLERS 36 SHOTS and in the same apparent
category another thing called CAJUN PAGEANT, a hexagonal explosive
wrapped in cheesecake art with the sum of all planes depicting some
sort of "bathing suit competition" in which each weirdly clad,
different-colored beauty contestant wears only a beehive hairdo
(with antennae? feelers?) in addition to her conical sci-fi costume
and robotic "poise" (that is, notably somber and unsmiling, without
attempt at the phony shiny regular-earthling-variety contest gri-
mace). CHEERFUL NOISE, SOUND OF MUSIC, MARDI GRAS PARADE.

❉

I remember that there were still kids staying throughout the sum-
mer and there was a big fireworks show on the 4th of July and for
our entertainment, Dad lit an M-80. He was a master sergeant in
the National Guard on weekends. We lived in the Old Superinten-
dency, or Building NO. 26. Every morning my mother or father set
seven bowls of oatmeal porridge on the table for me, my brothers,
and sisters (mine was always cold and rubbery and I was usually late
for school although I could easily run the eight blocks at the last
crucial minute). There was a beautiful antique mirrored bird's-eye
maple piece of furniture in the dining room that took up all a wall.
I did climb up to the ornately wood-carved mirror and wish and
wish that I could get inside it, like Alice, and did remain an unrea-
sonable person all my life. My mother sewed all our clothes, the
basement was full of fruits and vegetables in Mason jars. In the
kitchen drawers were some heavy stainless steel spoons engraved
with U.S.I.S. We were the only family in town who had a totem pole
in the front yard.

Across from our home was the Old Infirmary or U.S.I.S. hospital
building which was a grim and Dickensian affair. It was haunted.
Next to that was the Pocahantas Lodge or domestic science building
where girls learned to cook, sew, and iron. It is haunted. My desk
is in the corner, on the first floor and by the door. I have worked
upstairs alone many late nights next to the dark and narrow wooden
door where the ironing board folds out of the wall, because I had to.
A medicine man or woman is periodically called in to perform the
necessary functions, as is the Pest Control, but those little running
tapping presences never go away.

The early 1900s large white frame Pocahantas Lodge with the
dark woodwork and old sewing machines and bolts of fabric and
ghosts in the attic is now the Main Office. The superintendent and

administrative staff are in it. My desk is not too many footsteps from where I started out, in NO. 26, but sooner or later I'll move on again. From my desk I can see the round spot near the ceiling where the pipe to the cast-iron cookstove used to go. The floor is creaky anywhere. The upstairs has slate blackboards on the wall and a wooden wardrobe where the prom dresses used to hang. There was an annual Spring Tea to which town ladies were invited to see the girls' etiquette, dressmaking, and assimilation skills. There was a massive round oak table and chairs in the parlor, hand-carved by a master craftsman who taught the boys his trade. These and many other fine vocational education artifacts were beaten to splinters with a sledgehammer in the time of plastic metal furniture, since it was the government policy not to leave anything in a usable condition if it was to be replaced. The only school record I ever saw for my grandfather was a 1920 statement: "This boy is a very good citizen. There has been a lot of sickness in his family." At that time of the century entire families of Indian people had died from the WWI influenza epidemics. Many orphans were brought to the infirmary, among them my brother's father-in-law who came up from the Sisseton Sioux Agency in a horse-drawn wagon to the ambulance landing out back and "I never did leave the place" he said at his thirty-year retirement party the last year that the school was BIA.

BIA realty records show that the town cemetery was originally the property of the school. I called a retired employee to ask, and he answered that the land was deeded to the city "in exchange for perpetual care." There are no markers with the Indian or mixedblood names. One day the old-timer came in to visit, bringing an ancient yellowed cemetery record book, where he had found the name and resting place of a little girl who died in 1918 at the U.S.I.S. infirmary.

He took us to the unmarked grave which was tightly surrounded by the monuments of strangers. There was no way to guess.

❄

The gymnasium was named after Jim Thorpe, the Olympic hero of Carlisle Indian School. The girls' dormitory was named after Sacajawea, heroine of the Lewis and Clark expedition. The boys' dormitory was named after Tinker, a dead Indian soldier hero. When the federal-Indian bugle boy roused up the student population every 4 A.M., they put on their itchy wool soldier uniforms and drilled and performed on the sidewalk grid in front of the Pemmican mess hall, the Jim Thorpe gym, the dorms, and then they went to do their details in the barn or the laundry or the bakery. In his old age my grandpa enjoyed singing reveille tunes at breakfast. In his school days he learned how to barber, blacksmith, carpenter, cobble, dairy, garden, and write in beautiful cursive penmanship and write himself some books. The BIA flag with the bull bison standing in a sunburst that I used to see run up the flagpole every a.m. by Indian boys along with the stars & stripes is retired to the closet by my desk. The most decorated soldier in North Dakota history is a Sisseton Sioux alumnus and employee. Although dreadfully wounded in the Pacific, he left the medical unit AMA to single-handedly destroy a bunker full of Japanese. I recall that when he used to visit our house he had to communicate with my dad by means of hand signs, a tablet and pencil. The effects of his injuries must have been compounded by then and he was nearing the end of his life.

In the school library is a History of the Wahpeton Indian School book made by seventh and eighth grade students in 1941.

It is made of frail green construction paper, cardboard, pencil and crayon illustrations, and inkpen text that says *We find that the student body took an active part in war work during the first World War 1917 – 18, several students became soldiers in this war.* The school superintendent was given a promotion and sent to the BIA boarding school at Carson City, Nevada, but *During the big war times flu epidemic in 1917 or 1918 he contracted the disease and died.*

❀

A Pearl: According to the little dusty green book, *The barn was burned on April 24, 1923. It was started by a boy who wanted to see the new Wahpeton truck in action. He had sense enough to get the animals all out. The fire department did not get there in time to save the barn. The authorities did not find out who started the fire until six months later. Some boys told on him. He was sent to reform school because he had done many wrong things besides burning the barn. The barn was rebuilt on the old walls in 1924. They put a Gothic roof on the barn. It cost $11,300 to build the barn.*

The baroque silver-roofed brick barn was a creepily enticing place to climb around in, smoke cigarettes, play hooky. I had an incorrigible habit of truancy, so I ended up at the reform school myself. I didn't want to go to school anymore, I saw how everything was & always would be, I only liked books. My favorites were *The Adventures of Huckleberry Finn* and *A Narrative of the Captivity & Adventures of John Tanner, U.S. Interpreter at the Sault de Ste. Marie During Thirty Years Residence Among The Indians in the Interior of North America,* which answered the question of what HF might have found had he lit out for the Territory as he proposed to do in the end. These two books corrupted me. Assimilation was a real dumb idea, I was having none of it, not ever. When they finally let me out of my "room" to go to the canteen, I saw it was full of Indian boys and girls. I heard somebody say Hey! Right on, Pukkon! and instantly knew it was Turtle Mountain Chippewa and it was the ones I knew at Wahpeton. "So this is where the Indian School kids end up," I thought.

❁

On my initial do-it-yourself adolescent vision quest I heard the elm trees talking. "Aneeb. Aneeb. Aneeb." They never said a thing to me in English. A little while later, after I walked through the park and across the bridge, they were dancing on the levee, waving their arms wildly with the electric moon and velvet sky and winking toy-town lights and mumbling black waters behind them, I laughed. Nobody else could see this. Walking through the old campsite, I acquired a little helper. It looked like a small beadworked man glowing on the elm bark. I looked a bit closer and decided it was a cecropia moth larva or bookworm. Ha ha, I'm kidding! Meanwhile the sidewalk was made of these jeweled Alpha-Bits in various surprising colors running past like a flashing light message. I always saw the letters everywhere, every time although it remains a mysery what if anything was spelled. They were weirdly frosted, like some kind of changing metal cereal. The name Wahpeton in the Dakota language means "dwellers among the leaves." At my workplace the academic building is named Sequoyah Hall after the indigenous genius who invented the Cherokee alphabet or syllabary or "talking leaves." As for Walt Whitman, the Funk & Wagnalls says *In 1865 he became a clerk in the Indian Bureau of the Department of the Interior, but was fired by the secretary of the department on the grounds that* Leaves of

Grass *was an indecent book.* I never had the urge to jump out of high-rise windows, carve people up with a butcher knife, or writhe on on the ground screaming gibberish, you can do all kinds of crazy stuff on paper.

⁂

The reason I mention all this, is to pack up for when the time happens, a bundle of words for this convoluted journey. I have come and gone several times since the 1970s, and worked at the Wahpeton Indian School in different years as the "DHHS/PHS/IHS Medical Clerk, Typing" "Intensive Residential Guidance Counselor" and "Therapeutic Coordinator." It's something like the reservation: you can leave, but sooner or later you'll be back—a little remnant of acreage in the midst of the non-Indian town that has grown all around it, and what must serve the purpose of a village for too many Indian children when there is no one left to raise them but the grandmothers. The gangs. In recent years the boarding school has gone from BIA to tribal control. Owing to a 1994 act of Congress, the school now has "therapy" as its stated mission. The students I see now are often grandchildren of those who came here in the 1950s and 1960s. Some say the boarding schools are an obsolete system that perpetuates dysfunction—only a handful are left in the whole country. Others will tell you there is nothing else out there for the kids who don't fit, who get sent.

⁂

News Transmitter Reports Pink Thunder Chrysanthemum: As we leave South Dakota, the sky is a deepening blue we know to be a significant meteorological mood swing. In our rearview we see the cloud stuff swelling and piling high into a puffy mass that blots up the darkening stain of the sky. At the state line ahead of us, though, all is so bright and hot and clear I wish I could crack a couple of eggs on the scene and cook them sunny-side up. There is a historical marker, a white frame farmhouse, and yet another roadside fireworks sale in an old trailer painted bright red. In the trailer we buy an item called GLISTENING BUTTERFLIES. In the blistering heat we walk the ditch, heading back to the pickup truck, and I think I see JoJo the Dog-Faced Boy coming out of the corn but it would be not polite to take another look.

At the highway overpass by the square man-made lake and the national historic bonanza farm July 4 celebration, we spot an elderly Indian runner moving down the road across the fields, a neighbor whom we have spotted at different times running along in Massachusetts, Minnesota, South Dakota, Kansas, Washington, California, DC, or somewhere in Europe on CNN. We outrun the storm behind us, but at home the sky is wet and sulky and the fireworks show gets called off until the next night. Then it is completely dark out with no rain and it's up to us to make some sort of a spectacle: run and get the bug spray, popcorn, lawn chairs, beer, Kool-Aid, video camera, and string the colored Owl Party Lights through my apple trees that I found at a rummage sale this summer, still in their packaging.

To the south of us the stack of clouds was piling higher and higher, six miles up, which is the height of the atmospheric tropopause against which the clouds would spread out and flatten and attain an anvil shape or cumulonimbus or "thunderhead" formation. Not until the dark is complete and we begin our festive small disturbance do we see it: the monstrous flashing shape of the T-storm, blooming bright in the night like some violent carnation. The TV weather show doppler radar shows its location to be thirty miles away directly over the ghost town. Our thunder is stolen by the wrathful pink bouquet. Every time the lightning coils and strikes inside of the cloud its perfect textbook formation gets illuminated. We witness the terrible splendor of the T-storm, whose distant silence is only feebly challenged by town fireworks. Long after the microscopic effect of our paper and *gunpowder* contrivances are all gone and used up, we stand in the muggy smoking darkness slapping the onslaught of buffalo gnats and mosquitoes, grateful that the rain and winds and hail and electricity are being slung down elsewhere and it costs us nothing to watch.

❂

EMERALD METEORS, WHISTLING MOON TRAVELER WITH REPORT AND COLOR, MARS MISSILE, MUSHROOM CLOUD (19 SHOT WITH REPORT), MAGICAL SHOTS BARRAGE, DESERT AT NIGHT, COSMIC CELEBRATION ZENITH, REPORT GOOD ROCKET, 10 GUN-SLINGING SALUTE, SATURN MISSILE WITH CRACKERS, THUNDER THOR

❂

On the 4th of July in 1995, Boy #2 is in the hospital for a burst appendix, and the special color front page of the local newspaper features a USA rocket drawn by Boy #3 and the headline story with mugshot of the mixedblood girl who shot a man two nights earlier downtown and walked into the bar across the street and had a drink waiting for the cops to come and get her, another country-western saga. In the morning I looked down out of the hospital window and noticed a red boat beneath the footbridge, then a yellow crime scene tape and some frogmen and firemen and by and by the TV news cameras, state's attorney, local newspaper reporter, some joggers and dog walkers and pretty soon a gawking crowd. When the newspaper matron arrived she verbally challenged the state's attorney. "Mr—, are you talking to the Fargo stations and not *The Daily News?*" By 5:30 the Search and Rescue and Fire Department had given up their useless mucking about in the river and the attempted murder weapon .357 magnum revolver was not to be found. The shooter, a stranger in town, reportedly confessed to having thrown it off the footbridge before going to the bar. Wild rumors had circulated before the paper came out, even identifying a local Native American female teacher as the suspect. Police-band radio hobbyists were identified as the source of this false report. Some teenage girls on bicycles were still hanging around the bank in late afternoon watching the frogmen and firemen who were all eating sandwiches from the boat. "This is, like, the biggest thing that's ever happened around here," said a girl.

But, back in the 1930s the local bank was robbed by the Alvin Karpis-Ma Barker Gang who drove their getaway car down the dried-up river bed to South Dakota. Near the footbridge the river swirls over a "car dam" constructed in the drought years; at that time also, the Bois de Sioux was dredged and straightened from the White Rock Dam project almost into North Dakota. On a balmy, green day in May the waters below the dam are teeming with fish which draw a crowd of anglers, and pelicans. The sky is blue, blue with white clouds or pelicans. The grass ripples lushly over the banks and the pelicans in the water act like white sailboats with the breeze gusting them down the canal into the blue distance. The old man who lived across the street from us in a later part of Wahpeton was the bank teller who was pistol-whipped by Karpis. He used to back his long boxy automobile out of his driveway and clear across the street so bashingly that the curb had a bite in it. The lady bank teller who was taken hostage and shot in the escape down the riverbed was later on a retired schoolteacher whose inscription and signature I discovered in a discarded children's book brought home from the library, the book is a long illustrated odyssey about the life cycle and coping mechanisms of a hermit crab whose positive message is *Once more a new Pagurus, Pagoo, for short, had found his place in the endless rocking rhythm of the sea.*

TOP TEN FIREWORKS I NEVER SAW

1. CUSTER MASSACRE 61 SHOT NATIONAL HOLIDAY NOISE
2. DRUNKEN BEES 96-SHOT IAMBIC TETRAMETER & TRIMETER EMILY DICKINSON ORGY
3. MOTHER OF ALL BATTLES FESTERING SCUDS MALEDICTION
4. INTERMITTENT EXPLOSIVE DISORDER (WITH PEARLS & REPORTS)
5. ATTENTION DEFICIT DISORDER WITH HYPERACTIVITY BARRAGE
6. CONDUCT-DISORDERED BIRDS
7. KILLER DAFFODILS & SCREAMING BUDS
8. JIMI HENDRIX SKY PARASTHESIA EXPERIENCE
9. SEXUAL THOUGHTS BLOOMING HOLLYHOCKS ZENITH
10. PINK THUNDER CHRYSANTHEMUM WITH CRACKLING SILVER VOLTAGE

Indian Education Q & A of the day: Just as we're all about to finally leave the office for the holiday, another vexing drawn-out problem comes in the door and in a fit of exasperation I ask, "Why don't we just get a professional to do it?" and the stoic deadpan of the Arikara business manager, "Because we're Buy Indian."

Two Birds & One Stone: While I'm doggedly working on a long detailed report, the accountant asks, "How can you *stand* to look at all those words all day? I hate having to write anything, how can you stand it?" and I'm dumbfounded, thinking of the insane and never-resolved purgatory of scrutinizing numbers far into the night and empty haunted-office weekends and I say like a joke, "Easy, man, easy. It's both my sickness and my therapy."

The sky is full of smoky roses.

. . . Midnight.

※ ※ ※ ※ THIS HAS BEEN A GEOGRAPHIC MEMOIR, A REPORT FILED UNDER "SUMMER" WHAT I DID ON MY SUMMER VACATION 7-4-96 ※ ※ ※ ※ BANG ※ BANG ※ CRACK ※ ※ CRACK ※ CRACK ※ ※ BANG ※ ※ ※ ※ ※ ※ ※ ※

Gerald Vizenor

Excerpt from *Manifest Manners*

Native American Indian literatures have been overburdened with
critical interpretations based on structuralism and other social sci-
ence theories that value incoherent foundational representations of
tribal experiences. Brian Swann and Arnold Krupat pointed out in
Recovering the Word that structuralism, a "concern for principles of
organization and function," dominated their edited collection of
critical essays on Native American literatures. The "Indian as an
individual is not much examined in these essays."

Claude Lévi-Strauss and Alan Dundes have been cited more
than Mikhail Bakhtin, Jean-François Lyotard, or Jacques Derrida in
the historical and critical studies of tribal literature; the theoretical
persuasions have been more structural and representational than
postmodern in the past few decades of translation and interpretation.

Foundational theories have overburdened tribal imagination,
memories, and the coherence of natural reason with simulations and
the cruelties of paracolonial historicism. Anthropologists, in particu-
lar, were not the best listeners or interpreters of tribal imagination,
liberation, or literatures.

The elusive and clever trickster characters in tribal imagination
are seldom heard or understood in translation. Missionaries and
anthropologists were the first to misconstrue silence, transformation,

and figuration in tribal stories; they were not trained to hear stories as creative literature and translated many stories as mere cultural representations. Victor Barnouw, for example, wrote in *Wisconsin Chippewa Myths & Tales* that from trickster stories "we can learn something about the belief systems of the people." He misconstrued the trickster as "a real person whom they respected although they also laughed at his antics."

Barnouw reduced the oral trickster stories that he heard to unreasonable social science evidence and cultural representations; moreover, an analysis of the storyteller concluded that "there was evidence of emotional dependency and also some confusion about sex." This outrageous interpretation was based on a Rorschach record.

Karl Kroeber pointed out in *Traditional American Indian Literatures* that anthropologists and "folklorists, whose disciplines are not directed toward appreciation of superior artistry, usually play down, or ignore, the individual distinction of creative accomplishment in ethnographic material."

Moreover, anthropologists have used the inventions of ethnic cultures and the representations of the tribes as tropes to academic power in institutions. "The critical issue, so far as concerns the anthropologist as author, works and lives, textbuilding, and so on, is the highly distinctive representation of 'being there' that *Tristes Tropiques* develops, and the equally distinctive representation, invertive actually, of the relationship between referring text and referred-to world that follows from it," wrote Clifford Geertz in *Words and Lives.* "To put it brutally, but not inaccurately, Lévi-Strauss argues that the sort of immediate, in-person 'being there' one associates with the bulk of recent American and British anthropology is essentially impossible: it is either outright fraud or fatuous self-deception. The notion of a continuity between experience and

reality, he says early on in *Tristes Tropiques,* is false: 'there is no con-
tinuity in the passage between the two.'"

Native American Indian imagination and the pleasures of
language games are disheartened in the manifest manners of
documentation and the imposition of cultural representation;
tribal testimonies are unheard, and tricksters, the wild ironies of
survivance, transformation, natural reason, and liberation in stories,
are marooned as obscure moral simulations in translations.

Museum Bound

summer clownwinds
fold nations
places
narrow word lapels over whales

oral traditions
bacon fat
mouthwash broadsides
pleat the same tribal meadows

voice storms
thunder from isolation booths
dead seasons

temple mirrors
double faces from the darkness
crease the bathroom

concrete rivers
fastfoods and loneliness
slower at the corners

black squirrels
crows
mountainbears
sacred visions at the treeline
coin returns

summer clownwinds
wrinkle fools and nations out of time
unfolded
we are museum bound

Beaver
—excerpt from *Dead Voices*

October 1979

Turn the sixth card over at dawn.

Beaver in the wanaki circle, beaver in the north.

The beaver are with me now on this sixth turn of the cards. The stones are broken into beaver and land in the north. We are the beaver of chance, beaver turned over on the mountain wind, turned over on the cards. We are beaver on that slow burn at dawn, down from the wild treelines to our tribal agonies in the cities.

We are beaver on the run this morning, beaver from under the dawn. We are the river beaver, and our broad tails were once delicacies to the tribes. Then the wordies discovered our rivers and stole our stories and left us with their dead voices.

The gentlemen of the time wore felt hats pounded from our best hair. We were saved by the turn of fashions, a chance survival, but not before we were brought close to our woodland end by the fur traders. Now we find solace in the wild cities. The new fur traders are more obvious here, and our survival comes with stories not water.

The whole moon was brighter in the west just before dawn. We were out on the moist streets close to the treelines, a natural habit of beaver in the city. The snails moved deep in the wet grass. Flies circled in the first glances of sunlight to warm their wings.

Near that house with the blue heart a woman towed a miniature beast on a leash. We tried to hide but the curly beast rushed over the boulevard and pushed his wet nose in our crotch. His breath was rude and smelled of bad meat.

The woman was a nervous wordy and wagged her pure hands as she laughed, a practiced melody on the rise, and she pranced in the wet grass, but did nothing to haul her beast out of our crotch. We were certain the perfume she wore so early in the morning came from our stories, and it was probably castor, that familiar wild scent that confused the domestic beast. We took pity on him in the end, he could hardly smell the difference between a beaver and a nervous wordy. She must have been searching for a beaver. Why would she wear our scent so early in the morning?

"Fuss is confused over something," said the woman.

"Must be something, the early morning is so wild," we said. Fuss must wonder what his nose is telling him outside, are people animals or not, birds, bears, or maybe beavers? Fuss snorted with pleasure in our crotch.

Finally we smacked our tail on the grass and scared the beast. Fuss ran behind his wordy and pranced on her shoes. She said he could bark out the time, he was very smart.

"We knew a dog who called wingo at bingo games."

"Forgive me, but who is we?"

"We are beaver in the wanaki circle."

"Forgive me, but we are late," said the woman. She backed out of our conversation, turned on the sidewalk, and crossed the street in a hurry. The wordy and her beast were both very nervous. The beast started to shiver so she carried him the rest of the way home.

We were the beaver of fresh water who turned from the scented traps and landed in the cities to escape the fur traders. We were the water tricksters and dam builders, and we heard stories in the touchwood and luminous bearwalks that were natural at night on the great river in the woodland.

We were beaver and tasted the tender trees in the gardens on the block, a clean bite, not enough to leave an obvious wound. The live oak were on one side of the lake, hard and bitter, the incense cedar were smooth and mellow on the other side, and the palm were baked, dried, and tasteless. The bay laurel were pungent, the warm bottle brush tasted sour, and the mock orange had no taste that would ever be remembered. Nothing on the block could compare to the sweet aspen and birch trees near the great river.

The houses were brushed with dew, the stones carried leaves until morning, and the inside plants pressed on the windows to be outside in the autumn. The leaves carried their stories in an aura, and where the leaves have been there is a bright trace in the tree. The trace of an aura holds the natural shape of cut and broken leaves. How do beaver leave their traces in the water?

That big ginger cat sat beside the fern. He yawned and turned his whiskers on the breeze outside the basement window of a house near the middle of the block. The ginger had six toes on both front paws. The toes were his traces on the stone. The early sunlight cornered the dew on the low windows. The ginger watched the other cats as they posed on the rim and roamed on the block.

Several inside cats lurked beside the plants in windows, and others spied under porches and cars at the curb. Two cats howled on the fence in the garden at the corner. Some of the cats followed at a distance, they must have smelled our castor. Their gaze was wild, and the hair on their noses moved to remember the stories of the scent. We were beaver in the city and the cats heard the wild but could not remember the trace of our castor in their stories.

"Terrocious, this is absolutely terrocious," said the shrouded woman over and over. She turned over the cover on a storm sewer and shouted down into the dark manhole. "Come out, come out you nasty demons, come out into the bright light."

"Terrocious, what ever could be terrocious?"

"Terrocious, of course, a new word coined by combining terrible and ferocious," said the woman. She was older than the sewer, muscular, and her head was covered, but her hair must have been wild and white. She seemed to glow, but when we tried to see her face she moved her head down, or turned to the side.

"Do you live here?" we asked the woman.

"Not on your life," she shouted.

"Those covers are very heavy."

"Not really," she said, and shouted into the hole.

"Why are you shouting down there?"

"Don't be stupid," she shouted.

"Then tell us who's down there," we insisted and leaned over the manhole. Her voice echoed in the sewer, and we heard water and distant thunder. The cats were curious and one by one they came to the edge of the manhole. There, the big ginger laid his many toes on the rim and looked into the sewer. The other cats leaned closer to the edge. They listened and sniffed the foul breath from the dark and dangerous manhole.

The thunder could have been a summer storm, but the sound came from cars pounding over other sewers in the distance. We waited with the cats for something to happen, a withered hand reaching out from the sewer, a sinister voice, or at least an explanation from the woman who raised the grate and shouted to the demons in the manhole. Nothing happened, and when we turned the woman had vanished.

We heard her laugh and saw her turn the comer on the run. By the time we caught up to her she was close to the lake. The big ginger followed us but the other cats would not leave the sewer until something happened in the manhole. The sewer was covered later, but the cats continued to visit the site, the trace of the unknown.

Some cats peered into the small holes on the cover, and others pushed their paws down the holes. Nothing ever happened, but the cats took that sewer into their stories of the city.

The old woman picked things up on the path, feathers, leaves, and other bits of nature, as she walked around the lake. She was mocking our game, but we missed the play at first because we were so curious and hurried on her trail. At last she landed outside the empty crow cage near the lake and we had a chance to ask her once more about the sewer.

"You tricked us over the sewer," we told the old woman.

"Nobody ever tricks anyone."

"You shouted into that sewer and left us there."

"Nobody left you there," she said and turned her head.

"What was in the sewer?"

"Thunder, the water demons, who knows?"

"But why did you open that particular manhole and leave us there, and why so early in the moming?" we asked and tried to see her face. She wore a print dress, and a scarf covered her head and most of her shoulders. She carried a plain cloth purse, and when we moved closer she swung the purse to the side and drew the scarf over her face. The old ginger purred between our legs.

"Would you like to see my face?"

"Of course we would."

"Why me in the morning?" asked the old woman.

"Because, you seem so familiar."

"You see, my face could be a mirror.

"Easier to remember then."

"You wonder, could she be a trickster?"

"Who else would shout into a sewer at dawn?"

"Tricksters are stories not real people."

"We know those stories," we told the old woman.

"The trickster is a hand in masturbation, you can bet on that, the hand and stories are real, but nobody is there," said the old woman. She opened the cage, the same one the crow held until we rousted him, climbed inside and leaned on the wire. The old ginger followed her into the cage. "You heard the trickster and came to the sewer with your cats, but the trickster was you, not me."

"You are the trickster, we are beaver."

"Would you be a stone?"

"We are stones in our stories," we told the old woman.

"Come closer to the cage, come closer to me, remember me in your stories, remember you heard she was the old woman who was never there," she said and then turned to face us at the wire.

The old woman raised the scarf and died in a ball of light. She had a luminous head and the loose shape of a face. The light was bright, but there were no bones or real flesh on the face. The luminous head moved with colors as muscles would, and her eyes were dark and dangerous in the ball of light. She had covered the luminous stories of a trickster. The big ginger hissed at the light and ran back home.

"Naanabozho is my name," said the old woman.

"You have the same name as the trickster who created the earth, but how can you be here in a crow cage?" The crows cawed in the distance, and we might have told the stories about the crow who turned out to be a circus bear.

"Tricksters are stories, there are no tricksters but a hand in the night," she said and untied the ties at her waist, "Even so, you must remember me as a trickster, because who else can do things with shit that make people laugh so much?"

"Naanabozho made wordies out of shit."

"The trickster made the very first anthropologists out of shit," said the old woman. She raised her dress, squatted near the perch, and shit right then and there in the crow cage. "Now, let's see how many anthropologists we can make out of shit this morning."

Naanabozho had to be a wild figure in a trickster story or else no one would ever believe what she could do with shit. Trickster stories have been told since the stones and tribes were created, and we all know that the trickster made anthropologists out of shit, but who would believe that a real woman dumped in a crow cage and created a new school of anthropologists near Lake Merritt.

"Anthropologists end up in the sewers," said Naanabozho. She wiped her hands and tied the waist on her dress. Crows heard the shit stories and circled overhead. "What a waste, the crows and anthropologists never did learn how to shape and shift their own shit."

"So, is that why you raised the cover this morning?"

"No, there was nothing there, the sewer was a chance to catch cats and beaver over nothing," said the trickster. "My, my, and we caught the beaver of the day over a trickster sewer." She laughed and the wild sound burst from her luminous head. The crow cage was lighted, and thousands of cold insects rushed to the heat. Black flies circled her head in wide bands but no one ever touched the trickster. The heat was real to the crows and insects, but not the trickster.

"How did you know we would be there?"

"How could the beaver resist trickster creation stories over a sewer in the city?" asked Naanabozho. She had a new version of creation that turned the great flood into a sewer of anthropologists.

When the very first trickster was up to his nose in the great flood he asked some animals to dive down and come back with a few bits of sand so she could start a new world. The beaver and others dove down and one of them came back with enough for the trickster to make a new world.

Naanabozho told the new stories of creation in the city. "The last time we had to dive through shit shaped anthropologists to find the remains of the tribal world and create a new one," said the trickster. She smiled and there was a trace of blue light on her hands.

"So, we should dive into the sewer?"

"No, but a terrocious accident happened right there in that sewer," she said and leaned over a pond in the crow cage. There was no reflection, the water would not hold her luminous head.

"Get to the terrocious parts," we insisted.

"This is a creation story about a crossblood blonde with webbed toes who could swim faster than anyone in the world. She might have saved the tribe in the great flood. She was a cheer-leader, and on her way to school one morning she heard that seduc-tive purr and distant thunder deep down in the sewer and vanished in the manhole," said the trickster who had created her out of shit to tease the teachers. "Now, the school shaman heard that domestic cats were the only animals who could rescue the blonde, but her teachers were not certain that the cats would cut the shit to save a blonde.

"They were right, the cats, black, white, and calico, refused to wade into the shit in the sewer, so the trickster created an anthro-pologist out of shit, named him Shicer, a doctor in the new school of tribal care and rescue, and sent him deep down into the sewer to find the cheerleader."

"So, did he find her in the shit?"

"Shicer was very proud to be the first rescue anthropologist made out of shit, and the first to be asked to dive into the underworld of demon shit to save the crossblood cheerleader, the pride of the tribe in the city.

"Shicer landed at the bottom of the sewer and heard that distant thunder, the wild drums over the manhole covers, but he could not see the end of the tunnel so he touched his way in the thick water and whistled a happy tune from the new school," said the luminous trickster.

"Naanabozho asked the beaver to do the same thing at the creation after the great flood," we told the trickster. "The trickster was up to his nose in water, and his own turds floated close to his nose, so he asked the beaver to dive down and rescue the last of the old earth, but it was the muskrat who came back with a little bit of sand, enough for the tribe to pack a new island on the back of a turtle."

"Shicer had no such luck," said Naanabozho. "The blonde he found in the sewer held him so close that their bodies melted one into the other, and no one could figure out how to pull that shit apart."

"So, how did they get out?" we asked the trickster.

"What seems to be a game is not a game, the opposites are never the other, the plurals, even the pronouns we write, are not in the natural world, and one plus one comes to shit in a blonde and anthropologist, so we pushed the curious domestic cats into the sewer to separate the shit, and somehow that ginger cat with the six toes came back with parts of the pair," said Naanabozho.

"You mean the big ginger ate shit?"

"She shouted 'raise the cover and lend me a paw' and then climbed out backward with a double hand and two ears of shit in her mouth, and later she hauled out their melted heads," said the luminous trickster. "The other cats purred over the remains in the sewer, but the big ginger was the only cat that came back."

"What happened to their heads?" we asked the trickster.

"The blonde and the anthropologist became a mutant in their heat, a sewer creature of the city," said Naanabozho. "The big ginger sat there at the rim of the manhole and watched the crossblood head turn into a rescue anthropologist, and then their heads melted with the last of the webbed toes in the tribe, back into the sewer."

"So, are they the purr we heard this morning?"

"The tribal mutants purred and teased the demons in the sewers, and their sound became much louder and heated the corner," said the luminous trickster. "The big ginger knew the secret, and there were stories about the underworld of lost cats, but no one could figure out what caused the purr, or the light at the end of the sewer.

"Everybody knows that shit gives off a gas, and even more in this case, but no one expected that blonde and anthropologist to turn green and shoot a light out of the holes in the sewer cover," said the trickster. "That big purr and then the weird light at night started some incredible stories.

"The man who lives across the street from the manhole said he saw two white cowboy boots and a pink pony come out of the sewer and dance, and then a man around the corner told everybody that he saw a giant calico cat that glowed in the dark and ate dogs," said the trickster. "Other people told stories about giant cats, great balls of light, and thin demons in streams on the street down to the lake, but no one was too worried until people started to lose their hair and vision."

"The wordies were going bald and blind?"

"Yes, and people were scared so they called in the federal government to see what sort of tribal evil had been poured into the sewers that would cause wordies to lose their sight."

"How about getting old?" we asked the trickster.

"They were so taken with the purr and the light in the sewer that the wordies forgot their own stories about getting old," said Naanabozho. "They never had many stories to start with, so they were distracted by weird lights and purrs from the underground until they needed glasses."

"So, what did the government do?"

"They sent out two anthropologists who were experts on witchcraft to see what was the matter with the sewer," said the luminous trickster. "The two were fearless scientists, naturally, and so they climbed down into the sewer and never returned.

"Now, you might think, as many people do, that they were taken with the same blonde as the first anthropologist, but it turned out to be a bit more complicated because the two never knew they were fashioned out of shit until they were part of the underground, and once there, faced with their ultimate trickster origins, they embraced their own shit in the sewer."

Naanabozho was no more than a trace of light when we turned back to the crow cage. She had vanished at the end of the stories on sewer rescues and the crossblood blonde. She left behind her cloth purse, and when we leaned over to pick it up a crow bounced on our head and landed on the perch in the cage. Could it be that the crow we had turned into a flea and then a circus bear was back in his cage?

Later, we heard in stories told by a black panther that the bear, who was once a cage crow, beat his circus trainer with a bicycle, bit two children, ate three dancing dogs, and then became a trickster with a luminous head. She came back to the lake to haunt his enemies, the wordies, the beaver, and the old crow in the city. He ruled the sewers with shit demons and then retired once more as a crow in a cage.

Nothing has ever been the same since the trickster turned the blonde and the anthropologist into melted shit and dead voices in the city. Black flies and other insects have been sucked into the holes on the sewer cover.

Lake Merritt held the bright trees on the surface, and leaves floated over the broken water treelines. We rushed to the flea bench near the end of the lake and opened the cloth purse. Inside, there were buttons, twigs, feathers, seeds, two coins, and many stones taken from the path around the lake. The luminous trickster might have taken over our game if she had not tired and returned to his perch as a crow.

We were river beaver on the run back to our apartment. We circled the sewers on the block to avoid the odor of the anthropologists. Their shit could wound tribal children at night, and their demonic light could ruin our stories in the city.

The cats were in their windows, and the big ginger purred beside the tender fern. We turned the mirrors to hear the bears in our stories. In the distant light we placed one stone in the circle for each cat on the block, and the stones from the cloth purse became the wordies who turned to shit. The floor of our apartment was covered with stones. We are stones broken in the wanaki game.

Once we carved our beaver sticks from the sweetest aspen and birch to build our houses on the great river, and then we poked the shit demons back into the sewer, and set our sticks to purr in the wanaki circle. One card waited to be turned. We were beaver near the end in the city.

James Luna

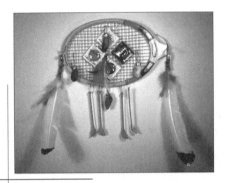

Wet Dream Catcher

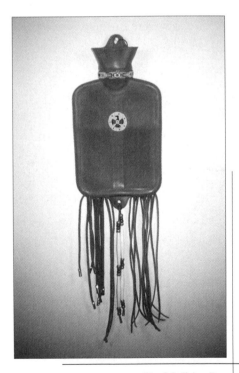

Hot Medicine Bag

You See What You Want

The Shameman

The Thinker

Guernica

Rosmarie Waldrop

from *A Key into the Language of America*

I SALUTATIONS

Are of two sorts and come immediatley before the body. The pronun-
ciation varies according to the point where the tongue makes contact
with pumice found in great quantity. This lends credence, but no hand.
Not so entirely Narragansett, the roof of the mouth. Position of hand
or weapon conventional or volcanic formation.

> *Asco wequassunnúmmis.* Good Morrow.
> >> sing
> >> salubrious
> >> imitation
> >> intimate

I was born in a town on the other side which didn't want me in so many. All streets were long and led. In the center, a single person had no house or friends to **allay excessive sorrowe.** *I, like other girls, forgot my name in the noise of traffic, opening my arms more to measure their extension than to offer embrace.*

the Courteous Pagan

barefoot and yes

his name laid down

as dead

one openness

one woman door

so slow otherwise

so close

VI OF THE FAMILY AND BUSINESSSE OF THE HOUSE

A solemne word, family, that no one trained to explore celestial mobilities would try to hinder. Not even a stranger. Above genus and below order. Covered with chestnut bark. They stow their families along diagonal axes and put their eggs in baskets, pigs in pokes. Prefer the movement of planets or buffalo to European **coatmen,** identifiable strains to city planning even when applied to lexical items. **Wetuomé mese. A little house. Which women live apart in,** the time of their exhaustive volume. Of the roundest. The aperture secured, so no eruptions may crash out of proportion. Or **long poles** on the off side of finance. Which commonly the men erect. Long neck and body. A longer house with a last stand.

> the other
> and its head
> sleep has no
> of mirth
> the fall

A procession, a river of people, the whole town crossed into exaltation to subject the body to their rites of candle and flame, cries and bewailing, mourning and evening. Could I withdraw from such offereing. I was not innocent enough to expect an end to hostility and housemaid's knee. A faulty birth no guarantee of entrance. Nature the more ruthless in getting back its chemicals. I rushed my headlong into it and found I made no splash. It would take a different kind of water to quench my long terror.

No one comes ignorant
among corners and stones
carrying beans
and a tune
and child besides

a stranger's
tongue they must yet do not
know
will twist their lullaby
their child their hand-me-down
their gums their genes their lovingly

Native Writings After the Detours

VIII OF DISCOURSE AND NEWES

Tidings on condition, a corresponding sign to sound which our geologists have discolored toward the vanishing point. Echo off yore, their preoccupation: **if white men speake true** or only to disturb the air. Even living in translation **they deliver themselves** at arm's length with emphatic purpose according to stress and position and sometimes alongside it. The message, slowed down by change of climate, becomes obsolete. **And understand not** that a tongue must keep in consonant motion to cover up its fork.

print

worthy

Pannóuwa awàun, awaun   Some Body Hath Made This
keesitteóuwin.   Lie.

Too long I took clockwork as a model instead of following the angle my inclinations make with the ground. **Why speake I not,** *I should have asked, counting on articulation of sound forms in waiting. The restless oscillations stripped me of more mythic aspirations and left my muscles mendicant, destiny manifest, skeleton without closet.* **When it is here, when it is come,** *alone or in a crowd, the moment always a matrix of terrible and stupid. My tounge so tied. To mother. Never as clear as when straight impulse bends back into curve.*

comes as
bait
where speaking
is still possible
the messenger
runs swiftly till
no
matter how
he can't forget

XII CONCERNING THE HEAVENS AND HEAVENLY LIGHTS

Which they adore, above acknowledging colonization. The stellar pallor attending powers shot madly from their spheres, the sky all over the earth, heaving its divine dimensions. If quickened circulation acts upon our thoughts, the moon so old it sets in full proportion. A light that does not slap you in the face, but raises nouns like navigation and transcendence. Nothing strange in pigment (black) that does not feed on side-stars obtained by imperfect combustion. Rocks. Meteorites. Great Western Railway.

> opalescent
> celestial
> celebacy

*An inner heat, an inflammation, predicting intimacies to hurt your eyes. Expanse of bodies, heavenly, observed on **lying in the fields**. Frequent occasion. And measured by their angle **much observe, in motion**, like the tin box tossed, sure curve belonging only to itself. Parabolas of the intimate, these very children will throw stones.*

> toward sunset
> the uninvited guests
> have guns
> and written off
> red skin

> they (mis)
> take territory
> from imperative

XIX OF FISH AND FISHING

Rising from sleep teeming with cold, bass, mackerel, salmon, whale and **Kaúposh. Sturgeon.** Yet a native **for the goodness of it will not furnish the English** with the praise they're fishing for. A hook in the throat. Cold eye on the scales. More of commerce than blind allegory. Some English **have begun to salt** as against native smoke the harsh reality. The soul eludes the bait. **Machàge. I have caught none.** Only puns, in **nets they set thwart** drowsy rivers in perfect passive voice, which will be shelled before the next May flowering. Explosive sky.

> fission
> fissile
> fiscal
> whistle
> risk

It was more in retrospect that net results seemed fishy. True, I had swallowed the most intimate head of a cold-blooded vertebrate. Then recollected tranquillility to counteract convulsive laughter. Which might fault me, like any Eve, with expulsion from paradise, or simply lack of hooks. But I was careful not to reveal my age or other unsure passage through the body.

> two-chambered hearts
> or even more alone
> big English will
> devour little fish
> length of
> tooth twice as natural
> as equal opportunity

XXII OF THEIR GOVERNMENT AND JUSTICE

Caunoúnicus, the elder Sachim, far removed from probability, lets his word stand upon the injury received, his inference more angular against the motivation. The sun also. Hardens. You cannot tell by looking at the sky that breaking laws must take place in the matrix of everyday thought, not a runaway amplification. Hence the Sachim either **beats or whips or puts to death with his owne hand** and foot since verse, too, is a form of government. There were 20-odd broken jaws given birthplace and enough (Eu)rope for hanging.

> juggle
> juggernaut
> jugular
> juvenile
> juxtapose

Did I only imagine people pointing fingers at me? No matter that I placed myself dead-center in their discomfort, they picked up the scent, whereas my lover was allowed ritual gestures even in the most traditional frame. If I had an aptitude for growing old, would I find objects worth my guile?

> dear reader, I've transgressed
> beyond the pale into
> yet whiter shades
> and all
> the elements lie
> evenly in periods

XXIX OF THEIR WARRE

Surplus valor comes as messenger and heaves ambush. **Shóttash.**
Shot. A word made from English though their guns come from the
French. A third arm. Liable to sudden deviation. Then he has against
him copious and pathetic voiced explosives to **kindle the flame of**
wrath of which **no man knowes how farre** it will branch to the right.
A wager on who drew the first bow, on how many slain, the barking
of a dog.

> predestination
> desert
> storm
> disability
> **Npúmmuck. I am shot.**

Year of parades. Celebrating exploits unsuited to my constitution. As if every
move had to be named expansion, conquest, trinity, and with American
intonation. The traces of the push across this continent and others no less
flagrant yesterday, but now enlarged with profit and consequence. Our own
private ceremony hardly enacted when it was all already over. Close up, my
flesh was dark, a dead end. My terrified lover left me. For his own likeness.

> I worried about capture
> in wars nobody hears of
> a prisoner
> in my own genitals
> that sum me up to some
> my **deep-down-in-the-forest**
> my troubled
> my self the self of others

Marie Annharte Baker

One Appropriate First

See slither me on approach to poet. See speak special cult jargon.
See grateful how when opportunity I hang out. Poet writes people
about who writes alike. I like this wait. Appropriate spoken word
must come out. His speech first then it is time to ask. Now is there
another way to ever think Native Americans are the ones you must
know the ones I mean I ask as no Indian Attack scheduled today.
Cartoon looks appropriate. Ugh, Rain-in-the-Face ask why whiteboy
not raindance in event cultural appropriation takes over secret ritual
chores with performance.

Gift exchange. Book of poems written by womanself.
Somehow he knows this. Write to: from: his everyday name from
my poet name. How one generous poet with suggestions says call
him *white boy coyote*. Right. Right. Boy his name is inappropriate.
Have to talk more soon. No more time to talk. Times back I didn't
know what to write about for whom for why. Wow! Cool! He said
thanks when I said *thanks*. Neato! We are participating in each
other for now!

This white boy coyote anticipates the question not asked. Should split in case his history is next. Hmmm yes. Hmmmm no. Native American woman writer said she is *artist first* then Turtle Island

Woman second. Could be I line up. His wife could sure obedient woman pose. Full lotus beside him in public. Her private squeeze nirvana and zen then dharma then hum out his first finger. His shell with echo is coyote cackle yowl after crisis in the chicken coop is over. Just his sayso as if *First Nations First* is what was never said in the first place.

'Rangutan Rage Writes About Story

She makes it all up. She writes who knows me. She makes up the stories. 'Rangutan stories. How she saw me hide all night in a library. Saw jealous husband chase me. She looks at me. Sees me lug books to bed. Hidden behind text I read. Her eyes reflect me sawed in half. Says a magician took the other half. What's left now for a medicine woman to devine? See our mothers are inside us. Ones who left us for men. For drinks. For laughs. Some are the popular aunties we visit for bannock and tea. They will become Old ones. Keep us company. Respect our time. Wounds. Sure got remedies. Preachy words. She watches me croon to dance drum. 'Rangutan beat on chest. Beat memories down inside the breasts. Because I keep forgetting. She's not that proud. The one who bears my wounds. Shame. Lust. She is buddy to my body. She reaches for the scars. Speaking to me that way. Moaning how the stab didn't quite do her in. She's lucky for that. Lucky she does feel a bruise. The one who wore the blackeye. Convinces me I am angry for nothing. She took the beating for me. I've got nothing to talk about. She's got it all. Keeps it straight.

Beware Writer

Walking home I notice all the Beware Dog signs. Does this mean Beware Natives Are Moving Into The Neighbourhood? Or, is the message Watch Out This Is The Tough Westend Part Of the City. One house has three Beware Dog signs. Does that indicate 3 dogs? Beware Three Dog House.

I notice the fences. Some are chain link. Most of the houses have run down fences which have Beware Dog signs. I see dogs in them. One is a puppy who doesn't bark. His huge chain has him caught by a kid's toy. He falls over on his back onto the plastic truck. He tries to right himself. Another dog sits at the window. Maybe longing to be outside. Another, a small collie runs up to his fence and barks excitedly. He is across the street and the owner is in the yard.

Between the houses that have Beware Dog signs I see a Native place now and then. The most obvious have their kids playing outside on the porch or veranda. Some little ones are quite noisy and don't look at me when I pass by. Some are just quiet and stare. One little girl who is very fair has a very dirty little face. She wears only a small pair of shorts. She plays with her plastic trike getting herself more dirty. She has her own yard. One little girl across the street is hauling two of her friends in a wagon through a vacant cement lot. Maybe the Beware Dogs are inside their houses so that these children might play outside for a few hours each day.

Maybe the German Shepherds, Rottweilers, Pit Bulls, and Dobermans are taking a day off. It is Sunday afternoon. It is their day not to guard a home or property. Burglars may also be taking Sunday afternoon to stroll around the city. Are they casing up the places to hit next week? At least, the dogs are not so evidently on duty.

Maybe everyone is afraid. I chose this street carefully. Looks residential. Mostly houses with kids playing outside. These houses have families. Hey, families must live on the streets I'm avoiding. They live in big run down blocks. Managed by one big outfit like an insurance company. These managers of the ghetto don't give tenant insurance or life insurance to the people who provide the salaries for them. Real overlords. Sure the name of the gang. The people who run the worst part of the westend have private, protected names.

Carolyn Lei-lanilau

Hawaiians, no Kanaka, nah Hahh-Y-in

—*for My Darling* Kūpuna, *the Beauties Aunty Bea and Aunty Kika*

(manohman—da hahdest subject to write about in my liiife)
Iknow I goin get buss up fo diss because eeeEverybody like be
ali'i, I only like be *kolohe.* Dis jess my story, no da bessest, not the
truest, jess mines.

Firs you gotta know my genealogy and dis buggah iss te hahdest.
I dunno my genealogy so much. I know I get distant Mākoleo-
kalani from *tūtū,* my
granma's sistah but to tell the truth, I jess not intereested. Maybe
because so late
to know
and maybe I scared to find out.

Question: just WHO is Hah-why-an?
I saw a definition by Ronald (in his pitch letter for his calassy publi-
cation) make the distinction of "colored"/"ethnic"—as oh sohard.
He referred to his holiday "giving" letter
addressed to All Colored Authors whom he referred to as "diverse"—
What??? You cannoT understand what I try-ing to say?
—How you think I felt when I got the letta and my linguistic beagle
mine was sniffing it out
and it jess sounded so fucken politie. iT Tried to be PC but it was silly.

So WHo iss Ha—Y—in?

Whoa man, I dunno.
As Ka'ai said, "You jess gotta be"
Sooner or lata, you goin find the one's trying too hard
It takes no effort to be *Kanaka* (of course, arguable)
You born that way, like it or not: if I had *nānā*, paid attention to my
pubic hair, I would have felt more comfortable to be *kanaha* sooner.

Lastnight while I was gossiping with my cuz about Derrida and
Hopkins—or ws it the other morning when we were discussing
"Mana or Money?" that I told her about my conversation with the
ancient poet K and our opinions about pubic hair. I said, "I should
have paid more attention to my pubic hair than the hair on my
head," whic historically ad been the "bob" or the "bun; the bun
or the bob"—no other styles.
When Katie, the woman who cuts my hair suggested that I cut it
the shape it is now in because
"It would make you look more dynamic."
I replied that I could not afford to be more dynamic:
"my husband would divorce me"—which he did.
But the point of this is that everytime I would cut my hair,
the person who cut the hair always said,
"You have natural waves in your hair."
When I would go home to Hawai'i, the combination of salty,
humidity, pollution, and my hair would make my hair what my
older daughter refers to as "cotton candy hair."
So now that the hair on my head looks related to the hair in my
crotch, I feel "together," "reassured," "belonging:" now I have hair
identity.

Or maybe, because I don't care about anything silly like my hair,
maybe I am just being Hawaiian! or at least *kolohe*   (please, vote)
I dunno.

When I was a young kid and was carried around te market in
Chinatown, all the butchers would reach out their greasy hands with
a chunk of *char siu* all the while adoring my eyebrows and sigh
"Gahn liang."
"Bee-u-to-ful, beautiful eyebrows," the old folks would echo.
What? did this all mean?

—that I was so ugly that I Had to have SOMETHING attractive
about me; after all, the rest of my life, I was identified as being
"stupid and ugly." —Like when you ask someone
"What does he look like?" and they translate
"Ugh ly buggah" to "Shee has a wonderful personality."
When I check my eyebrows in the mirror, I can only wonder
"Is there ssSooo much *mana* in my eyebrows?"
The Hawaiians never mentioned anything about my eyebrows.
Must be a Chinee thing.

People have been checking out my hair NOW because it is so weird.
People say
"What's going on with 'the' hair?"
I say anything I want:
"It's making its own decisions."
"It's *tros* Hawaiian."
"I'm going through my menopause."
"I'm in love," which could easily slip into "I'm gonna kill myself."

The lovely lady at Tom's Fortune Cookies where I always buy my
chocolate fortune cookies yesterday said to me (in Mandarin of course)
"You hair look good. You look ten years younger."
Nodding her own ead in agreement with herself herSelf repeated.
"Look good," but I heard
"Look yaahhhyyaHHaaaghounnnnng hon-ney
Look hot! baby."
Without a thought I said,
"It's from eating all the chocolate fortune cookies."
And she smiling really did look beautiful; what she doesn't know is
that the more I visit her, the more Hawaiian she is becoming.

[The section on Hawaiian is dedicated to Mike E. FunMahn
(so I can write off my legal fees) because he always asking me
"So whatye doing for fun lately?" (So here's the answer man.)]

What then, Is Hawaiian?
Well, you have to know the postmodern Principle of *Pauhana* which is
based on the ancient proverb of ʻŌkole est ʻŌkole est ʻŌkole.   (vote)

Lynn was so excited as he sat next to me at the Templebar when
I searched for my pen to scribble "The Principle of *Pauhana*" as a
note to myself. The point is that Hawaiians know how to *pauhana;*
"in the *koko,*" the blood, as we say. Unlike *Haole* and *Pake,* and
Japanese, when *hana iss pau, Kanaka* no like still worry and work
some moa. We like to clear the desktop ass it were. Sooo many
times, it was *pauhana* time and the people around me were on
Tokyo or New York Stock Exchange time. Why? no need.
On Sunday, Lynn and I was singing and singing and laughing real
loud. We bruned our eyes staring at the ripe flesh of the *hula* dancers

who were doing bad-kine Las Vegas style *hula*. I said to Lynn
"*Aye,* dye we-ing underwea-ah?"
Lynn said
"Either they have a G-string or have wrapped themselves at
strategic points."

You should have seen it: the fat rolled up and over from all sides of
the bra.
The *'ōpū* wass talking: it said "You like feel?"
Throughout it all, the *po' o* of Ka Nation was not amused. Such a
pleasure not be in the position of authority. I loved it and all the
pleasure was based upon my *'ōkole* which was comfortable sagging in
the bar stool. When it came time to sing Don Ho's big hit
"*E Lei Ka Lei Lei,*" a very politically incorrect song, I knew all the
words and felt like I was still in the sixties when the song came out.
I got off the plane from my first year at college and when my girl-
friend arrived to pick me up, ALL the way home Carol Menezes'
naturally flipped hair was see-sawing back and forth, her body sway-
ing while she was humming "Ra-che-cha-cha-cha-cha-cha *e lei ka
lei kei.*"

[Here is the secret of life (the part of the book where people have to
send $50.00 to a secret address to get the secret): if you have missed
the Principle of Fun (on earth), then you have blown the human
experience. What then?
Go to hell.]

Ka mea Ka mea Ka mea Ka mea Ka mew Ka mea
(this, why? that, how? whatever; when?)

Hawaiians living and breathing on today's planet now and then eat French fries; have little interest in vertical formation and time management—no mo dah verbs "to have" or
"to be" ass why.
We have to *lomi* a lot and kiss kiss kiss.
I love the Hawaiians. I love feeling Hawaiian—it's just so everyting.

I love Hawaiians; sometimes they burn me up. You know, it's that sacra-mon(e)y of tourism *haole* kine ways that screw up the *na'au*— what I translate to mean, vision.

On the other hand, I just practicing English, man.
Why should Hawaiians be burdened wit being the perfect Paradisian? Whenever I speak to my friend Lokelani, I start out by asking the first question on every tourist's mind.
"How is paradise?"
Sometimes we evaluate "paradise," *en français avec a peu dōlelo o Hawai'i. De temps en temps nous parlons en anglais avec beaucoup de français academie.*

Why should I write only about the Aloha parade stuff.
The Chinese were furious when I wrote about their evil small sides that you don't see up front when you go to the Chinese restaurant and eat that dee-licious food that makes you feel like you entered the Middle Kingdom above the earth and below heaven. Not being biased I don't feel any more sanctimonious about the Hawaiians although I do have a bit more *aloha* for us *Kānaka.*   (vote, 1996)

We going out in style. Maybe we will cry more tan we can imagine because sometimes we just like a good one—man we *can* cry with that *hupekole* nose runn-ing and not ashamed.

You should see Aunty Nani cry. Lyrical. Adiago. Ballet. *Kupuna* can
drop crumbs on the tablecloth as she nibbles her bread and cioppino
And with her pinkie—class act, man
                              haole bettah watch and listen to this—
Aunty with her pinkie pick up those bread crumbs that look like
gentle rain showers,
the flower shower trees of gentle
Hawaiian is always making love (not only just the sexual kind but
the) *hā* and more hah, muscular, the physical heart like transubstan-
tiation of the bread
and wine and Mark got it too . . . in Kamau'u's writing rrright in
Blossom's eyes
Just when you don't expect it, it pops up in John Ogao
who is Puerto Rican Filipino and
There in Hanale's yummy body found in Morgan's wise and sweet
tongue.
Davianna doesn't show it right away because her *mana* too powerful
but little by little she will share he *mana 'o* and her sweet voice.
It is in Uncle Walter's smile—his silence and him always blessing the
food—how many times we sat in the restaurant and prayed.   VOTE!

If you was Hawaiian, you would cry-smiling or maybe you need to
hear it in my voice . . .
To be Hawaiian is to be very emotional because we love it.
Oh boy, Hawaiian is the greatest. *Nō ka 'oi!* The best.
Why you think the *haole* and Japanese like own our land?
Why you think they like have sex, marry us, and get da land
easy way?

Kūkā kūkā kūkā kūkā:
Of course, no one prepared anyone to be disciplined by our *ʻaumākua.*
How did we know? *Nānā,* pay attention all the time.
No one gave us permission—to ask questions? *ʻA ʻole.*
No one told the United States government to cut off da kine jets
from our uncles and beat
up the ladies that like talk our sweet *ono ʻōlelo.*
Me, I'm one bloodhound: I like act out my frustration
kupale, defend
correct, *pololei*
maybe appear to behave like an *ʻōkole* until I find out Why and How
things work: *hula*

I asked *kumu* (Naomi Kalama) about our *aloha.*
I confessed that it was so hard to be "natural" and to *mālama* every-
body /everything. Too many people don't know that it is so natural
for us to be nice.
Kōkua: to be present and helpful
Pono: to be in balanced with the gods and the natural world
Lōkahi: to be in harmony
Laulima: many hands working together

"Nice" is never enough for the non-*Kanaka* because
"the Other" always want "more" and not even Just More, because we
are so good at giving
and hospitality and and and, MoRE is stretched to impossible
dimensions and then
ʻaumakua and only then *ʻaumakua* must show a sign of *ʻa ʻole.*

I hate this analytical part of me. Too bad I not one scientist, yah? *Ono*-mouth Hawaiian as I am, I just went with my nose that led me to the good *wale wale,* the nutrients.

"Hasa manana, hemo de pajama."
Diversion. Diffusion. Nah, nah. Joke, joke.

laka, diety of the hula
E kala mai ia 'u, forgive my crass interpretation of your art.
This is my *hula,* my *cyberhula,* my virtual reality *hula,*
my wrong *hula* that draws attention to
the *pilikia hula* that so many lost souls are leading and more lost
souls are following.

Ono Ono Girl's Hula is danced on the keyboard in front of the monitor. My *kumu* is my sister Lokelani, *haumana,* student of *kumu hula* 'Iolani Luahine.

Our *'ōlelo* is horizontal and vertical simultaneously so as the in-house *waha nui,* I render the full, true, and slightly crazy offering of the story.

The 1996 registration form for the Native Hawaiian vote reads
Ho 'okūkulu he aupuni hou
Nāu nō e koho   i mua
To build a new nation, The choice is yours

Ha'ina 'ia mai ana ka puana   *(Let the Story Be Told)* circa 1893

VERSION 1 A CONTEMPORARY EXPLANATION OF THE TERM "*KAONA*[1]"
His "lani" in Lei-lani was gesture/
sketch of time between Lili 'u-o-ka-lani's [2] body and
the red earth striping its juiciness.

The structure of naming hinted blues, fire.

Not to question: apotheosis
or openly rescue morning dew.

Without "having" or "being" upon their tongues
'Ōlelo o Hawai'i [3] flowered into

white skirts, black ties

dry
stretched throats

gloves

belts

shoes that dug into ferns, kicked *koa* trees for durability;
measured land as ownership.
Shoes that dragged mud into the *hāle*[4]

pinched, the shoes scorned the sleeping heat.

One of the new items was books
that designed the course which
honored flower.

Pua

plumeria,

lehua, rare yellow and common red from the Big Island

mokihana from Kaua'i

complex and volatile *pīkake* and the cousin *pahalana*

kahili, white, violet, shell, torch ginger

lokelani, rose of heaven for Maui

kaunaoa for Lana'i

kukui for Moloka'i

Oahu's royal *ilima*

maile

hānai[5] carnation

hinahina for our beloved and bombed Kaho'olawe

limu kala[6] in rites for ocean *'aumakua*[7]

sweet potato vine on nursing mothers
necklaced around the born and unborn *kamali'i* to pump
nectar from the nipple

Roadside,

spring from roof between hair and ear

curving along breast into the waist with sea mist

in the pupil bathing

taste like mountain apple reflecting heart:

Ahupua'a—from sea to mountains
Lei-lani,
flowers and heaven
in rocks, lizards, owls and the wind,
an understanding

Kanaka maoli.[8]

'Ōkole[9] sweet
Lei-lani. Bone and flesh expecting like a fishnet.
Or the sugar that forfeited its
life transformed into profit—

vertical or horizontal guarantees that
earth was flat.
Expired, a soul transferred to heaven or hell.
In a box, the body rotted.

Not the common flower
her mother carried these petals over fire.

Shaved *lei* from *lani*
Gathered her skin for sharks
Revealed bones to secret.
No tears or illusions.

Adapting
the father counted money without interruption;
while her sister, herself already rock or fire.
How could a mother behave except pray?

And then,
inspite of the plantations and pineapple fields,
the tourists
and military,
Hawai'i never became the 49th state.

Eventually, *kanaka maoli* were named "Hawaiians" who
in English were understood as "those who
watch television wearing masks with sleeping eyes."

White bread was good-eating
sure enough:
the blue eyes had arrived and "the possibilities were endless."

---

1 *kaona:* hidden meaning.

2 *liliu ʻokalani:* Hawaiʻi's last reigning *aliʻi* monarch.

3 *ʻŌlelo o Hawaiʻi:* to speak in the language of *kanaka maoli.*

4 *hāle:* house.

5 *hānai:* adopted.

6 *limu kala:* seaweed garland.

7 *ʻaumakua:* this is a complex phenomenon commonly known as *ʻaumakua ʻohana.* This reference to the family spirit which was the combined efforts of all past *ʻaumakua. ʻohana.* While your *ʻaumakua* could be gentle, it represented order and could provide out-of-body experiences to educate and discipline any family member that was not behaving in family style.

8 *kanaka maoli:* Native Hawaiians.

9 *ʻōkole:* buttocks.

VISIT TEEPEE TOWN

Circa 1993

VERSION 2 WHEN LAND IS BROKERED LIKE PORK BELLIES
Lani of Lei-lani is body:

pulse of blood between Lili 'u-o-ka-lani's heart and
sky.
Lei-lani, Lili 'u-o-ka-lani: from heaven;

breasts, birds, hair, nectar.

'Āina, the land spirited
eyes and muscles into

lei.
A sacred ritual: dance.

Lei-lani, in human form
translates from 'Ōlelo o Hawai'i.

(Immigrants formed from crooked throats
drawstring tongues
wrapped in death
covered fingers
whips

bundles of paper called books.

The new gods stared into and at bodies while asleep toward their
own devils.)

Seaweed, *'opihi,* and mullet multiplied.

Bluefield, apple and spider bananas ripening
warm, wrapping one leg around another.
Leading lips to sing. Lips for ears.
Lips to eat.
Lips to tell the story.

Behind the palms and gardenia bushes,
inside the wood houses and openly
the ghosts uttered the written words they were born with
"obedience"   "abstinence"   "penance."

Pagans noticing clouds
the brown folks laying
laying laying while time endured their heavy bodies!

Here was opportunity: a project.
The *haole* could redeem himself.
He and she set to work.

E ha'awi, e ha'awi lilo
"Share. Give away the wealth"

the hymn urged strictly.
I kou mau waiwai,

"Share. Share."
Huli a hahai mai ia'u

I loaʻa i ke ola mau ia ʻoe
"Turn. Follow me
and live life forever.

—That was the promise.
Still, the body withered without
the skin shaved from bone;
flesh offered to *ʻaumakua.*
ʻAina had no tears or illusions.

The birds continued nesting.
Pīkake and ginger sweat the air.
The brown folks quilted their story in song and dance.
But the air heavier, the body sagged.
Nobody utters the reckless

no shame talk.

Everybody felt it—only felt
this belt, a girdle. This harness, a wrench, this yoke
a vice—these words, the papers, rules. The Order.

—Who could articulate
identify

express the loss of

the way the muscled walked
the way words surfed on tones.

express the loss of

the way the muscled walked
the ways the words surfed on tones.

As bicultural participants, egos formed.
In experiment and innocent of
this type, this process.
The sacred *hale* evolved into "shack."

Silence—the way ghosts feel clean—
sanctuary.

The elements performed reasonably—at first—entailed God.
God in *maile* slipping onto *lehua* rising into sun god

God in the holy birds that died for the *ali'i*
ruling cape.

The temperatures were perfect for God.

Paradise:
Nobody hid a body in clothes.

Male and female were reliable specimens
and
especially cordial.

The gentlemen at Plymouth Rock were a bit
off course: but, indeed
this stretch of beach

the artesian wells and
lovely soil
were promising:
there were possibilities.

Barbara Tedlock

Pilgrimage
—excerpt from *The Beautiful and the Dangerous*

Under a swollen lavender sky a crowd of men in black blankets and
white headbands appeared along the western horizon. As they
approached I could make out the leader of the masked dancing
society, his warrior priest, and the leader of the Coyote Society;
behind trailed forty Good Kachinas, the ten Koyemshi or Mudhead
clowns, and dozens of pilgrims.

Scrambling off my rooftop perch, I raced across the street and
jerked open the front door—momentarily arresting Tola's corn
grinding. Seeing that the old lady had been crying, I decided not to
blurt out my news just then. I was confused by finding her this way
and didn't know if I should enter or not; if so, should I, or should I
not, offer her comfort?

I slipped back outside and leaned against the cool stone wall,
tensely at ease. I gazed at the ten silly-looking, but nonetheless
sacred, serious, even dangerous, Mudhead clowns. Adobe-colored
beings in tight-fitting cotton masks with inside-out eyes and dough-
nut-shaped mouths, simultaneously expressing eternal amazement
and voracious hunger. Ears, antennae, and genitals (stuffed with
hand-spun cotton, garden seeds, and the dust of human footprints)
protruded knoblike from their heads. Without noses or hair, they
were naked except for lumpy orange-brown body paint, feathered

ear ornaments, black neck scarves, men's woolen kilts, and women's blanket dresses, concealing their tied-down penises.

Loooong ago, these clowns were created when a priest sent his son and daughter to locate a village.[1] The children ascended a mountain, where the girl became drowsy and lay down under a cottonwood to rest. Her brother went on looking all around the countryside, then returned at midday to find her sleeping soundly. A delicate breeze lifted her skirt; he became enchanted, lay down beside her, touched her, slept with her there.

When she awoke and realized what had happened she became enraged, tore out her hair, and beat her face and head till lumps appeared. Screamed till her lips turned inside out. Wept till her eyelids became unsightly puckered swollen rings. Babbled unintelligibly until her brother, unexpectedly, began to understand her and they changed their language there.

And when they changed their language, the boy said to his sister, "It is not good for us to be all alone. We must prepare a place for others." He descended the mountain and drew his foot through the sand, creating the Zuni and Little Colorado rivers. Where they converged a lake was formed, and in the depth of that lake the village of Kolhuwalaawe/*Kachina Village*, the Land of the Dead, came into being.

That night the girl bore ten sons; all but the first were infertile and, like her, deformed. Each had a distinguishing personality trait and a sacred gift for humankind.

Molanhakto, with a miniature rabbit snare dangling from his right earlobe, brought native squash. The Speaker, a daydreamer who rarely spoke, and then only irreverently, carried yellow corn. Great Warrior Priest, a coward, brought blue corn. Bat, in his black blanket dress, who feared the dark but saw marvelously well in daylight, red corn. Small Horn, who thought he was invisible, white corn. Small Mouth, the glum, gabbling and cackling constantly, offered sweet corn. Old Buck, frisky and giggly as a young girl, black corn. Gamekeeper, in his woman's dress, speckled corn. Water Drinker, always thirsty, toted his water gourd. And Old Youth, the self-centered, thoughtless adviser of the team, brought the clairvoyance locked tightly within the tiny cracks in parched corn.

I hear a muffled shuffling of mud-red bare feet, goat hooves rattling against turtle shells, and jingling abalone on shell-bead necklaces, announcing the arrival of Kokk'okshi/*Good Kachinas*. Kachina chief and spokesman, dangling netted gourd jars filled with sacred water, lead the dance troupe—in their turquoise-painted wooden masks with slit eyes and long black horsehair beards, zigzag lightning streaks across their clay-pink shoulders—into the earthen plaza.

Clustered behind the masks come dozens of pilgrims with white pants, white shirts, white headbands, and white face paint meandering across noses and dripping down cheeks. Their bulging knapsacks wriggle with turtles. Fistfuls of cattails jammed into black leather belts. Hidden among the masks is Sadie's eldest son, thirteen-year-old Shawiti, this year's Fire God, carrying a juniper-bark torch in his right hand.

Pounding bare feet, cracking of dewclaws on turtle shells, trembling painted gourds, whining growling bullroarers, followed by song:

Aa-ha ee-he aa-ha ee-he
hiya elu [joy] *naya elu* [joy] *it's our day*
"Oh, this is our happy day
Come out with your rain,"
the North Priest says to his younger sisters.
Hiya [surprise] *hiya* [surprise] *lii-lhamm* [here-mm]

"Oh, this is our happy day
Come out with your rain,"
the North Priest says to his younger sisters.
Hiya hiya lii-lhamm [here-mm]
ohoho elu [joy] *ohoho elu* [joy] *he'ahi*
ohoho elu [joy] *ohoho elu* [joy] *he'ahi*
ahahaha i-i-i-hihi hiya [surprise] *hiya* [surprise]

*

Aa-ha ee-he aa-ha ee-he
hiya elu [joy] *naya elu* [joy] *it's our day*
"Oh, this is our happy day
Come out with your rain,"
the North Priest says to his younger sisters.
Hiya [surprise] *hiya* [surprise] *lii-lhamm* [here-mm]

"Oh, this is our happy day
Come out with your rain,"
the North Priest says to his younger sisters.
Hiya hiya [surprise surprise] *lii-lhamm* [here-mm]
ohoho elu [joy] *ohoho elu* [joy] *he'ahi*
ohoho elu [joy] *ohoho elu* [joy] *he'ahi*
ahahaha i-i-i-hihi [surprise] *hiya* [surprise]

A chorus of half-turns and sharp pauses follows, the shaking of long black horse-tail wigs over a medley of gray and red fox furs, with dangling fluffy tails, and skinny hind legs inches from the ground. Yellow parrot feathers bounce on the crown of each dancer's head; long black rain beards sway across each male kachina's chest. Six female kachinas, all but one danced by a male, dressed in their single-shouldered black wool blankets and double-pinwheel maiden hairdos, hurl piercing falsettos through rain words as they spin the lead dancers, twelve future Shalako maskers each marked by a two-foot-long glimmering military macaw tail feather.

> *Hapii-me hapii-me*
> *Rainmakers come to our sacred water bundles hiya lii-lhamm*
>   [surprise here-mm].
> *Rainmakers come to our sacred corn bundles hiya lii-lham*
>   [surprise here-mm].
>
> *ohoho elu* [joy] *ohoho elu* [joy] *he'ahi*
> *ohoho elu* [joy] *ohoho elu* [joy] *he'ahi*
> *ahahaha i-i-i-hihi hiya* [surprise] *hiya* [surprise]
>   *
> *Hapii-me hapii-me*
> *Rainmakers come to our sacred water bandies hiya lii-lhamm*
>   [surprise here-mm].
> *Rainmakers come to our sacred corn bundles hiya lii-lham*
>   [surprise here-mm].
> *ohoho ela* [joy] *ohoho elu* [joy] *he'ahi*
> *ohoho eln* [joy] *ohoho elu* [joy] *he'ahi*
> *ahahaha i-i-i-hihi hiya* [surprise] hiya [surprise]
>   *
> *Aa-ha ee-he aa-ha ee-he*
> *hiya elu* [joy] *naya elu* [joy] *it's our day*
> *"Oh, this is our happy day*
> *Come out with your rain,"*

the North Priest says to his younger sisters.
Hiya [surprise] *hiya* [surprise] *lii-lhamm* [here-mm]

"Oh, this is our happy day
Come out with your rain,"
the North Priest says to his younger sister.
hiya hiya [surprise surprise] *lii-lhamm* [here-mm]
ohoho elu [joy] *ohoho elu* [joy] *he'ahi*
ohoho elu [joy] *ohoho elu* [joy] *he'ahi*
ahahaha i-i-i-hihi hiya [surprise] *hiya* [surprise]

The Mudhead song gently filters through, whenever the Kachina Society song is soft, like something seen through the windows of a passing train:

We emerge from fourth inner world.
Carrying our grandchildren
we emerge.

On my back
staring in six sacred directions
sits my poor grandchild.

Hurry
call for rain
poor grandchild I
carry.[2]

The singleness of purpose of the dancers, pilgrims, and clowns marks them off from the surging crowd. With four sets repeated in the four plazas, their danced prayer opens the Flour Cloud Season.

Off Torn Place Plaza, House Chief sits within the northern kiva all alone, in total darkness on the cool earthen foor, chewing his sacred root, talking silently with songbirds. Maskers and clowns dance his heart along jeweled cornmeal, rainbow, and star trails, carrying him back to that time, long ago, when the earth was so soft that water was gathered simply by pulling up grass. Arriving at the beginning, he dreams life-giving thunderheads, lightning, and big-drop rain into a gemstone sky.

That evening we drove Tola over to the north side of the village to visit Sadie in her subdivision home. The cramped stucco frame house, painted canary yellow in order to distinguish it from the row of nearly identical Housing and Urban Development (HUD) houses, was unbearably hot, although all the windows were wide open. The kids, trying to cool off, were alternately running to the kitchen sink to splash themselves with cold water and panting like Siwolo/*Buffalo,* their shaggy black dog.

Sadie apologized for the intolerable heat, explaining that she had never really moved in. They didn't much like the place; it had plumbing but, unlike the older Zuni stone homes, it was divided into many tiny rooms, making it a scary place to sleep. So they used it primarily as a bathhouse.

She and her mother had decided to tear down the big stone house in the center of the Old Pueblo and build a new house on the same spot. In late fall, after the Shalako house-blessing ceremony, she would move into the new house with her mother and leave the subdivision house to her younger sister, Flora, or else to whichever of her kids married first.

The door opened soundlessly, revealing her barefoot husband in his pilgrim's pure white cloths and headband. He held out his right hand toward his mother-in-law, with his fingers curled downward, and said something.

Gently meeting his down-turned right hand with her up-turned left, Tola replied, "Le' happa/*The same.*" After hooking fingers lightly, for just a moment, they withdrew to breathe from their hands.

He turned to Sadie, then Ramona and Seff, greeting them each in the same manner. Removing his cornmeal pouch from his right shoulder and looping it over a forked tine on the rack of his first buck, he lowered himself stiffly into his favorite easy chair. Tola and Sadie returned to their butchering, and the kids to their games.

Homecomings are often approached gingerly, which leaves the returning male, if at all talkative (and most are), disconsolate. On this occasion Sabin solved his problem as his father-in-law had many times before, by talking with us. Actually he didn't exactly talk with us so much as he talked aloud to the room.

He spoke slowly, with many pauses, while staring straight ahead, with a glazed look, at nothing.

> We went all the way over there to Kachina Village Lake.
>
> Saw some of them
> what do you call 'em with white marks?
>
> Antelope.
>
> You can't drink water on the way there or on the way back
>   if there's no rain.
>
> Lucky for us
> there was rain
> on the way back.
>
> Shawiti
> is Shalaawitsi
> Fire God this year
> so he couldn't drink anything the whole time
> until it rained.

Native Writings After the Detours

When it rained
it rained hard
really hard
and that rain smothered out his fire

We called him
Ky'a Shulaawitsi

Water Fire God.

I used to ride a horse
when I was a kid but
I stopped when I was in high school.
I'm not used to it.

When it rained we had to force the horses to come in.
I got sore.
I didn't take any warm clothes.
I got cold.
You walk and walk and walk and walk
then you ride a horse and someone walks in your place.

If the bosses ran you run
so you've got to be in shape.

On and on you go until
you come up on a high place and
just see more country streeetching out.

Then you go on until you come to a high place again and
    you see more country.

There were a lot of new barb-wire fences we had to cross and
lots of windmills out there.

One of them wasn't working so good
it didn't look like there would be enough water for a cow.

That's a bad sign for next year.

We went way up on Fire God's mountain and
left our feathers there.

Shawiti had to make fire with his drill.
He did it right off
so as you know his *kuku*/father's sister *loves him*.

I went down into that cold muddy water and
got some of them drown children
you know
turtles.

There were lots of
cattails—

Guess you saw them in the dance?
We went way inside the cave into that fourth inner chamber
and it was dry.
Dry.
Bone dry.

Guess we'll have another bad year.

On the first day we got aaaall the way over to someplace
    on the other side of St. Johns Highway.
We spent the next night over there.

Then we woke up
way early in the morning
and walked all the way to Ojo Caliente.

It rained really good with good lightning and good thunder.

When we got to Ojo Caliente
Mother came to feed us
and we spent the night there.

When you go over there
it's like going to Zuni heaven.

He went on to explain that tonight would be something like Shalako. The dancing would start late, at midnight or so, and last until dawn. Tomorrow, in late morning, they would dance in each of the four plazas.

"Where's Kwinsi, and Shawiti?" Dennis asked.

"Don't worry 'bout them. They had to spend some time in that Longhorn house. Kwinsi will be back in a couple of hours, but Shawiti won't be home for a couple of days—not until they wash his sacred paint off. Poor little fellow wasn't allowed to ride a horse, and even though I massaged his feet about an hour, each night, boy, they are sure swollen!"

Standing up awkwardly, he walked across the room and stood at the kitchen door, where his wife and mother-in-law were butchering a sheep. Sadie had her arm way up inside the carcass and was working away on the ribs with a small hacksaw. Her porcelain tabletop rippled red with spread-out mutton.

I suggested that we might take a picture of Sabin—for history and all—maybe with Sadie and Tola, sitting around the kitchen table. Sabin smiled and nodded but Tola said sternly, "No, out there in the front room."

With an audible sigh Sabin stood up, putting his white head-band and cornmeal pouch back on, and walked over to the vanity mirror. While adjusting his headband, he explained that he couldn't wash his muddy feet or remove his face paint till it was all over, tomorrow evening. He stood next to his favorite deerhead trophy for two full-length portraits.

In the first photo, a gleaming-white electronic blur bounced back from his glasses. The second, without glasses, revealed a blank red-eyed stare. Pictures no one loved, liked, or even wanted. Technological failures revealing the insistent documentary urge to freeze, store, and retrieve the authenticity of an encounter with a returned pilgrim. Examples of ethnographic bad faith.

1 For fuller renditions concerning the birth of Koyemshi/*Mudhead* clowns see Cushing (1896: 401 – 3) and M.C. Stevenson (1904: 32 – 34).
2 This Mudhead song (part of a song string), performed once every four years when the pilgrims return from Kachina Village, is my translation of the Zuni text collected by M.C. Stevenson (1904: 68).

Native Writings After the Detours

tj snow

(Untitled)

and for the faint of heart (I). will be brief, to suppose the writing in proposing the written. Writ. And again the formulation of placation toward erasure. (I) am writing.

One question: Can you escrape the page?

Several words specific sufficiently random folds. upon internal. streeted turn torment on a fold enter. section. wallows residual. bill hit a bus in downtown traffic. a car lessens, the rapture. of placable. waste—race writing tends to be angry, one prof says. turns light blue.

❁

I light inwards into machinic, resembles wrote, elasticized written, enslaving, don't eat the fries, or can't wait really—

Several lines later, into presences. promontory ejaculant, respecting light blue notes of indians to open saves her torment, the later pressures of retrospective dioramas, heavy musk on catalytic floor—the ends of line, a bordertown scram. Hinge moments layers pages new.

Question 4: does the line?

*Phenomenology is the reduction of naïve ontology, to the activity of a *life* which produces truth and value in general through signs. But at the same time without being simply juxtaposed to this move, another factor will necessarily confirm the classical metaphysics of presence and indicate the adherence of phenomenology to classical ontology. . . . It is with this adherence that we have chosen to interest ourselves. J. Derrida. *Speech and Phenomena: And Other Essays of Husserl's Theory of Signs.* Northwestern University Press; 1973.

Furniture replaces dimes in the lobby, through the shore. fine line. comments consensuality
(on all those damned people written in my head.

In the position of the line, the range into image. Pictorial shit. crude,
westernized, interpretation of my indianness, oops, anger. A fine line.
These shadows puppet ledger scrawl out of floridian enslavement.
Rhymes, really.

A torment, has generations. of questions (what number is this?

❀

Steward slave. stompers in chaosmos what shaman postridie transsucculent indian
indentifies. Wait in the car.

Replaces Image—Question?

From the politics of headlights, and poor visibility, echoes of midnight through
the centerfile. rolled. with a stable. Through the middle (_) have not held

the emergent everyday, gentrified bi-polar

so   antagonism, continual. commensurate.

words

haven't any spurs? Eper ons raised to full   soon another desires replacement

for scandalous swallows of land in the

harness shudder, ridden with zeal.

couldn't be a crusade.

The world in which an act or deed actually proceeds, in which it is actually accomplished, is a
unitary and unique world that is experienced concretely; it is a world that is seen, heard, touched,
and thought, a world permeated in its entirety with the emotional volitional tones of the affirmed
validity of values. the unitary uniqueness of this world . . . is guaranteed for actuality by the acknow-
ledgment of my unique participation in that world, my *non-alibi* in it. M.M. Bakhtin. *Toward a
Philosophy of the Act.* (Trans) Vadim Liapunov. University of Texas Press; 1993.

Native Writings After the Detours

Some

That is precisely why deterritorialization, in this kind of science, implies a reterritorialization in the conceptual apparatus. Without this categorical apodeictic apparatus, the differential operations would be constrained to follow the evolution of a phenomenom; what is more, since the experimentation would be open air, and the construction at ground level, the coordinates permitting them to be erected as stable models would never become available. G. Deleuze & F. Guattari. *Nomadology.* Trans. Brian Massumi. Semiotext(e); 1986.

To return. Instable. Unistable. Restable. Hide. And like never before. Myth criticism

words

Jakobson never reminds

Opulence mends sacrilegious sign walls maybe. Words into wonder. Half same.

Lags to recover. Court knows, Iago, huh? The beginning last

have

written, has layers, writ, writing.

Somewhere in the place of words lies. Object resumes location. turns indentity on a spit. Reminders. No one validates what that's been—weathertop storm of changes into history the sight of air and name-as-was-in-remembering. Foreign. Lies (resorted) engenders, he says, shifting sites   atone by allmeans buoyancy.   vert. clinging dizzy.

effortless

Lifts rise   Gotten to—even better signs leaf or muledeer reprise—
got to even if   in the common touch holds only. Retried. The resort storm greasy worm lies verb vein upon bodus in two segments with anal tract spreading. somewhere secular. What semes engenderation.

Once a surprise is always.

described

Storm secretes plural shift. Compromises warning, every good
humanist knows. inelemental steam. born.

Often legitimate.
My ancestors have no cause. for
concern. said. into quotes. and meth.

Who sings into morning. Says.

No template apprehended. In
colonizing
verbs. Shit. More anger. effuse.

I cannot green. Blue and green. Cannot said the first was apprehended
in context. Or hails causality, after.
one quaint pellative integer (or not causal?) Rustic poetic.
But arrests.

For stability mime. What pig anyway Juris i'm saving
for next near. Or pushing tomblike into sediment.
settles. anger.

❁

rolls up the spine. race. t
urn. to you. your turn. nger

❁

Hollow

enter prized full rouse recompress leaven ornament. for a time marks.
assiduous tines couldn't trail contain, hardly a catachresis could.

more than lesions   in
genuine concern

more then often left   sentenci

crane look
half same
covered in writing   ng

a little more dimension, tension, into layers
interspersed with *history I*—archeology is talking to dirt.
    Quantitative the sight goes pipeline burst. layers marlboro's early
    frozen north. for templates reason sad   worm engulfing the
    median captives. Source of light. Tastes *homo*. Replaces image.
When morning word.   contains, its surgery. And north empties savior.

Memoria   has vision of context. angry. winsome words.

    Or strident quotient calling. into beginning. The salient stays. of rock.
    a whole corner. banned, its tongue. to respondant (I)
                squash takes ride on corpuscules to hit. back
                wash. double hit. morning.

Dole open re:sold residual context of even the site of execution. Penetrates
                diorama i. causal.
                i. as indian causative
                indian as i.

Linda Hogan

Germinal

Downstairs, things are growing.
Down stairs to the cellar
guinea eggs have quickened
and grapes have turned to wine.
Lye is burning through its tub
near potatoes with pale shoots,
and the molds are dividing
in jellies beneath wax,
that underworld
beneath the house with its bad family,
that world below
drumming
like old women
and blood stirring in the neck,
the older world
with its pale, thin roots of grass
and all things saved and growing.

What Has Happened to These Working Hands?

They opened the ground and closed it around seeds.
They added a pinch of tobacco.
They cleaned tired old bodies
    and bathed infants.
They got splinters from the dried-out handles of axes.
The right one suspected what the left was doing
    and the arms began to ache.
They clawed at each other when life hurt.
They pulled at my hair when I mourned.
They tangled my hair when I dreamed poems.
As fists they hit the bed
    when war spread again throughout the world.
They went crazy and broke glasses.
They regretted going to school where they became so soft
    their relatives mistook them for strangers.
They turned lamps off and on
    and tapped out songs on tables,
    made crosses over the heart.
They kneaded bread.
They covered my face when I cried,
    my mouth when I laughed.
"You've got troubles," said the left hand to the right,
    "Here, let me hold you."
These hands untwisted buried roots.
They drummed the old burial songs.
They heard there were men cruel enough to crush them.
They drummed the old burial songs.

Pillow

There are nights with feathers underhead
I put an ear down
and listen for the voice of god
to rise up from the ticking.

Longer nights, I hold the pillow in my arms
like a lost child dreamed to life.

These feathers know the death rattle
of birch trees in white winter.
They roosted there alive one summer.

Pillow, please forgive us the bird's lost life,
I smell it still,
my face against the singed dark,
and forgive us our other trespasses,
the mice within our poisoned walls,
the infirm in our beds,
and refugees driven in snow like rabbits
chased by a circle of beaters.

In this narrowing life, let us come apart
and float off
light like feathers
carried altogether in air
and coursing dark rivers.

Even the mountains have broken open
with light
while businessmen lean forward
peering in.
Light is breaking forth
from stone.
It shines out
touching all the perfect creases
of their hats and greatcoats,
and even white teeth
and bootblack shoes.

Elk Song

We give thanks
to deer, otter,
the great fish
and birds that fly over
and are our bones and skin.
Even the yelping dog at our heels
is a hungry crow
picking bones wolf left behind.
And thanks to the corn and trees.
The earth
is a rich table
and a slaughterhouse
for humans as well.

But this is for the elk,
the red running one
like thunder over the hills,
a saint with its holy hoof dance
an old woman whose night song
we try not to hear.

This song is for the elk,
with its throat whistling
and antlers
above head and great hooves
rattling earth.

One spring night, elk
ran across me
while I slept on earth
and every hoof missed
my shaking bones.

That other time, I heard elk run
on earth's tight skin,
the time I was an enemy
from the other side of the forest.
Didn't I say the earth is a slaughterhouse
for humans as well?

Some nights in town's cold winter,
earth shakes.
People say its a train full of danger
or the plane-broken barriers of sound,
but out there
behind the dark trunks of trees
the gone elk have pulled the hide of earth
tight and they are drumming
back the woodland,
tall grass and days we were equal
and strong.

VISIT TEEPEE TOWN

The History of Fire

My mother is a fire beneath stone.
My father, lava.

My grandmother is a match,
my sister straw.

Grandfather is kindling like trees of the world.
My brothers are gunpowder,

and I am smoke with gray hair,
ash with black fingers and palms.

I am wind for the fire.

My dear one is a jar of burned bones
I have saved.

This is where our living goes
and still we breathe,

and even the dry grass
with sun and lightning above it

has no choice but to grow
and then lie down

with no other end in sight.

Air is between these words,
fanning the flame.

Those Who Thunder

Those who thunder
have dark hair
and red throw rugs.
They burn paper in bathroom sinks.
Their voices refuse to suffer
and their silences know the way
straight to the heart;
it's bus route number eight.
They sing all day.
They drum
and at night
they put on their shawls and dance
thundering on wooden floors,
the feet saying
no more
no more
and those on floor number one
who are scrubbing
put down the gray cloth
and beat on the tiles. Take notice
we are done
with your scrubbing
and gluing together your broken stones
and putting the open sign
around the neck of night
and bolting the sun to save your warehouse
from thieves and crooks.

You could say the sky is having a collapse,
you could say it's our thunder.
Explain to the president
why I am beating on the floor
and my name has been changed to
Those Who Thunder.
Tell him through the storm windows.
Those are fists he hears pounding.
Tell him we are returning
all the bad milk to the market.
Tell them all
we won't put up with hard words and low wages
one more day.
Those meek who were blessed
are nothing
but hungry, no meat or potatoes,
never salsa or any spice.
Those timid are sagging in the soul
and those poor who will inherit the earth
already work it
so take shelter,
take shelter you,
because we are thundering and beating on floors
and this is how walls have fallen in other cities.

What Gets In

In daylight
houses expand
like chests of majors.

In the dark night
they contract.
Don't be afraid,
it is only the house
breathing out
its daily war
with termites and slugs.

When walls and floorboards creak
we're afraid
of what gets in, light
from the next house
lying prone on the floor,
ten o'clock news,
a cat, wild
from the woods
and full of seed
stealing in the cracked door.
Even a child
from one night of love.

No place is safe from invasion
and everyting wants to live,
even the moth
with eyes on its wings
flying in on light.

And upstairs, bats are listening
with all their dark life
to what we can't hear,
to life and matter
in the eaves.
In true dark
the sound of wind arrives
all the way from stars
and dust from solar storms,
all the life wanting in,
even the moon at the window.

Wendy Rose

Subway Graffiti: An Anthropologist's Impressions

1 NEW YORK CITY, 1978
Day-glo signs of survival
in impossible places
the City
and we primates
consider our position
with full-armed pitches
through the holes
in our future.
We have not been here long enough
to know if there's a reason
to mate. We may be extinct now
as we tunnel through rock,
crush cockroaches
whose record is stronger
and longer than ours.

       Words on subway walls were cries of help
       arrangements made
       treaties abandoned
       death threats
       turned into rumbles
       with name and number
       recorded.

VISIT TEEPEE TOWN

Art starts
pragmatic
becomes design
     dies
     unseen.

2

My California-born senses
feel the subway
as an earthquake
strangely regular;
I grip the seat
and wait to see
if I should stand
in a doorway or duck
under a table.
     Reality is changed
     from three thousand miles.
     About this earthquake writing:
     fifty feet into island rock
     the people rumbled
     into each other,
dueling for power.
The slippery cliff walls
tell of war, of prayer,
of hunts long over
into the night, of idleness,
of romance, of dripping water,
of scurrying rats, of fires

generating on the ties
and dying, of logical regular
metal-slick strokes
returning through evolution
to basics.
        I can't read most of it.
        Style is now design
        and the messages remain
        secret, hieroglyph
        not hieratic.

Manhattan has no Rosetta Stone
in the earth to be found
and deciphered
by my probing
colonial tongue.
Train by train,
station by station,
they are
an underground blur.

3

$$$$ Hunger, engraved shells
        that will feed the deer
        who shelter in my belly.
        I will give you the ocean currents
        if you will salt my rotting meat.
        I will kill the rabbit for you
        if you will make it warm my feet.

I worship what I kill
I worship what I eat
I worship what it means
F—M.A.E. A blow for mankind
　　　　　upon womankind.
　　　　　From the bruises on your flesh
　　　　　you will give me a son.
　　　　　With the hand that wrestles
　　　　　a digging stick to earth
　　　　　you will grasp and I will dig
　　　　　all the deeper with my seed.
　　　　　The weak are to be run over
　　　　　by my rod of power;
　　　　　always we must know who is stronger
　　　　　by the broken bones of my women
　　　　　and my boys.
DUKES RULE! Our leaders
　　　　　eat themselves bare.
　　　　　They will not plant,
　　　　　they will not hunt.
　　　　　They are wasteful
　　　　　yet they sharpen their tongues
　　　　　on my labor. Not they
　　　　　but something greater
　　　　　keeps peace in the village
　　　　　or lets it go.
　　　　　These ones trade wives for manioc.
　　　　　Macaw feathers for turquoise;
　　　　　their power is bound to flesh
　　　　　and they are always
　　　　　always hungry.

STRIKE! Obsidian breaks
under elk antler.
Flakes, fingernail-shaped,
spin to my feet.
This is shaping,
this is ruling, this is eating,
this is organizing, this is symmetry,
this is god, this is copulating
this is real, this is to be defined,
this is beyond description.
We will defy
what we need
and we will be the shapers.
SCORE   Our language is precious.
These signs mark our clans
as we are dried
from where we emerged
to this place chosen for us.
We speak, we watch, we sing for signs.
We torment, we tease,
we will not let you hear the words
for they are sacred.
This is who we are;
we are the words.
You may someday hurt us
with the parts left behind,
words that were left
vibrating on the ground,
parings of hair, toenail,
spirit and song.

VISIT TEEPEE TOWN

For the White Poets Who Would Be Indian

just once
just long enough
to snap up the words
fish-hooked
from our tongues.
You think of us now
when you kneel
on the earth,
turn holy
in a temporary tourism
of our souls.
With words
you paint your faces,
chew your doeskin,
touch breast to tree
as if sharing a mother
were all it takes,
could bring
instant and primal
knowledge.
You think of us only
when your voice
wants for roots,
when you have sat back
on your heels
and become primitive.
You finish your poem
and go back.

Maurice Kenny

Oroville High, California

I can't believe I'm eating a cheeseburg
in Oroville, CA, where dogs yelp at ghosts.
What I can't really believe is eating
the cheeseburg in a classroom at Oroville High
among students taught the mastery of printing.
They're ambivalent to instruction,
indifferent to machines which will record
their births and local football games . . .
machines which are indifferent to Oroville
itself, the buttes beyond the town's
rigid limits where Ishi clawed rock desperately
struggling to preserve his unrecorded songs;
a school where no student knows nor cares
about the almond groves nor the gold
that built Oroville, let alone
Ishi's drum, nor the crisis of extermination,
not even their own.

Archeologist

Out of a sandy field
of wild strawberries
he kicked up
an arrowhead,
and his foot
bled.

Sweat

Bathtub
might well
run red
like an
Indian's scream

The knife sits
close to the dirty
water

Feet and calfs,
thighs and testicles
dare to slide
into the depths
of hell
observing the Ivory soap
float

Framed flowers
from Geronimo's
Oklahoma grave
hang above
the tub in triumph

Paul's
pink water lily
floats
and is the reminder
of so much death

The room is freezing
from the steam
rising out
of the waters

The foot lifts
the toes smile
to see there are still
five

You remember how
Hilary a Jew
hid in the closet
upstairs
from Hitler
bolting the door
from inside

This should be enough
to soothe and change
the waves of thought
the waves of scalding
water lapping
first the testicles
then nipples
at the edge

Lie still
and the shiny waters
will reflect

the tears
it has caught
consuming
history and old age
approaching

Is there a doctor
in the house . . .
as there is no view
from this tub

Smell the sweet
strawberries
of June
scent the delicate
iris

Red screams
grow louder
echoes
beneath the waters

A bubble floats
with Jim Morrison
Chief Pontiac
and the French
mad with revolution.

The blood rises;
the knife clatters to the floor.

Reading Poems in Public

I stand on a stage and read poems,
poems about boys broken on the road;
the audience tosses questions.

I tell of old chiefs swindled of their daughters,
young braves robbed of painted shields,
Medicine Man hitting the bottle;
I chant old songs in their language
of the Spirit in wind and water . . .
they ask if Indians shave.

I recite old stories,
calendar epics of victory battles,
and cavalry dawn massacres on wintered plains,
villages where war ponies are tethered to snow . . .
and they want to know
how many Indians commit suicide.

I read into the microphone,
I read into the camera,
I read into the printed page,
I read into the ear . . .
and they say what a pretty ring you wear.
The tape winds, the camera reels,
the newspaper spins
and the headlines read:
Ruffian, the race horse, dies in surgery.

At the end of the reading they thank me
go for hamburgers at McDonalds
and pick up a six-pack to suck
as they watch the death
of Geronimo on the late show.

I stand on a stage and read poems,
and read poems, and read . . .

Hachivi Edgar Heap of Birds

Monetish

Want

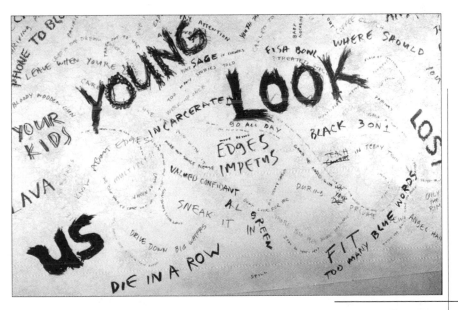

Young Look

BIG WHITE TEXAN

HOW

PUMP

THIS

HOLE

BOUT

ROPE THE KIOWA

THEM

VISIT TEEPEE TOWN

RIDE THAT WICHITA

COWBOYS!

Ma-ka' ta l-na'-zin

Allison Adele Hedge Coke

The Change

Thirteen years ago,   before bulk barns   and
fifth gear diesel tractors,   we rode royal blue tractors with
toolboxes big enough   to hold a six pack on ice.
In the one hundred fifteen degree   summer
heat   with air   so thick with moisture
you drink as you breathe.
Before the year dusters sprayed
malathion over our clustered bodies,   perspiring
while we primed bottom lugs,
those ground level leaves of tobacco,
and it clung to us with black tar so sticky we rolled
eight-inch balls off our arms at night   and
Cloroxed our clothes for hours and hours.
Before we were poisoned   and
the hospital thought we had been burned in fires,
at least to the third degree,
when the raw, oozing hives that
covered ninety-eight percent of our bodies
from the sprays ordered by the FDA
and spread by   landowners,
before anyone had seen
automated machines that top and prime.
While we topped the lavender
blooms of many tiny flowers
gathered into one,   gorgeous.

By grasping hold below the petals
with our bare, calloused hands
and twisting downward, quick, hard,
only one time,   snapped them off.
Before edgers and herbicides took
what *they*   call weeds,
when we walked for days
through thirty acres   and
chopped them out with hoes.
Hoes,   made long before   from wood and steel
and sometimes (even longer ago)
from wood and deer scapula.
Before the bulk primers came
and we primed all the leaves by hand,
stooped over at the waist for the
lower ones   and   through the season
gradually   rising higher   until   we stood
and worked simultaneously,
as married to the fields as we were to each other,
carrying up to fifty pounds of fresh
leaves under each arm   and   sewing them onto
sticks four feet long on a looper
under the shade of a tin-roofed barn,   made of shingle,
and poking it up through the rafters inside
to be caught by a hanger   who
poked it up higher in the rafters   to another
who held a higher position
and   so   they filled the barn.
And the leaves hung down
like butterfly wings,   though
sometimes the color of
luna moths,   or Carolina parakeets,   when just
an hour ago   they had been
laid upon   the old wooden

cart trailers pulled behind
the orange Allis-Chalmers tractor
with huge, round fenders and only
a screwdriver and salt in the toolbox,
picked by primers   so hot
we would race through the rows
to reach the twenty-five gallon
jugs of water placed throughout
the field to encourage   and   in attempt to
satisfy our insatiable thirsts
from drinking air   which poured
through our pores without breaking
through to our need   for more
water   in the sun.
Sun we imagined to disappear
yet respected   for growing all things on earth
when quenched with rains called forth
by our song   and drumming.
Leaves, which weeks later,   would be
taken down and the strings pulled
like string on top of a large dog-food bag
and sheeted up into burlap sheets
that bundled over a hundred pounds
when we smashed down with our feet,
but gently smashing,
then thrown up high   to
a catcher   on a big clapboard trailer
pulled behind two-ton trucks and
taken to market in Fuquay-Varina
and sold to William Morris   and
Winston-Salem   for around   a buck a pound.
Leaves cured to a bright leaf,
a golden yellow with the strongest
aroma of tobacco barn curing

and hand grown quality
before the encroachment of
big business in the Reagan era
and the slow murder of method
from a hundred years before.
When the loons cried out in
laughter by the springs and
the bass popped the surface on
the pond, early on, next to
the fields, before that time
when it was unfashionable to
transplant each individual baby plant,
the infant tobacco we nurtured, to
transplant those seedlings to each hill
in the field, the space for that particular plant
and we watched   as   they would grow.
Before all of this new age, new way,
I was a sharecropper in Willow Springs, North Carolina,
as were you   and we were proud to be Tsa la gi
wishing for winter   so we could make camp
at Qualla Boundary   and Oconaluftee
would be free of tourists and filled with snow
and those of us who held out forever
and had no CIBs would be home again
with our people, while the BIA forgot to watch.
When we still remembered before even the Europeans,
working now shoulder to shoulder with descendants
of their slaves they brought from Africa
when they sold our ancestors as slaves in the Middle East,
that then the tobacco was sacred to all of us and we
prayed whenever we smoked and
did not smoke for pleasure   and
I   was content and free.
Then they came and changed things

and you left me for a fancy white girl
and I waited on the land
until you brought her back
in that brand new white Trans Am,
purchased from our crop,   you gave her
and left her waiting in a motel.
The nearest one was forty miles away,
but   near enough   for you
and   for her   and I knew   though
I never spoke a word to you
about it,   I knew and I kept it to
myself   to this day   and time   and
I never let on
until I left   on our anniversary.
I drove the pick-up
down the dirt path   by the empty fields
and rented a shack for eighty dollars,
the one with cardboard windows
and a Gillespie house floor design,
with torn and faded floral paper on walls
and linoleum so thin over rotted board
that the floor gave if you weighed over
a hundred pounds.   I did not.
And with no running water of any kind,   or bathroom.
The one at hilltop,   where I could
see out across all the fields
and hunt for meat when I wanted
and find peace.
I heard you remarried
and went into automated farming
and kept up with America.
I watched all of you   from the hill
and I waited for the lavender blooms
to return   and when it was spring

even the blooms   had turned white.
I rolled up my bedroll,   remembering before,
when the fields were like waves on a green ocean,
and turned away,   away from the change
and corruption   of big business on small farms
of traditional agricultural people,   and sharecroppers.
Away,   so that I could always   hold this concise image
of before   that   time   and it
floods   my memory.

Dog Road Woman

They called you
grandma
Maggie   like
Maggie Valley
I called   on you
for your knowledge
of pieced cotton
I worked clay
to pottery
and thread   to weave
but   had no frame
nor understanding
of pattern
in quilting.
Climbing high
in sacred wood,
which feeds   the
di ni la wi gi   u no do ti,
I captured hickory
twigs   you wanted
for a toothbrush
to dip snuff.
Ninety-two year old
leathered fingers
caressed stitch
and broadcloth
into blanket.
You with your apron
and bonnet
and laughter
at *gold dollars*
and processed meats.

You who taught
me to butcher
without waste
and who spun
stories   on your
card   whenever I
would   listen,
we fashioned stars

Wokiksuye

—*in borrowed language in honor and memory of Bill Ice*

Like a horse's tail
so thick, black
down past his waist
beautiful.   Wanyaka.
Chemotherapy—
white man's
man-made cancer . . .
doesn't distinguish
between good or bad
cells . . . just kills.
The spirit is connected
to the hair at the
crown—pahin hocoka.
The hair falls
the spirit goes,
the will is
connected no more.
Leukemia—
cancer of the
White
Blood Cell.
Lakota wicasa
Oglala wica
Ha Luta Oyate   wicozani sni
Kuja, unsika
Canku Wakan o mani
ma wanagi o mani
wasigla
ceya
wokiksuye
wokiksuye

wopilamaye
miksuya
Canku Luta o mani
Canku Waste o mani
wohitika
iyomakpi, iyomakpi
ake—anpetu
anpetu waste
I knew him well.

The Year of the Rat
—*for Vaughan and Travis*

bu-bon-ic plague: a contagious disease characterized by
     buboes, fever, and delirium

for days sirens hurl winding shrieks
bubble lights flashing   red   yellow   red
yellow   white   linen
sheets   no,   drapery
rises and settles on
the feet   no, the
hands are pulling it
back again   "can you
hear   us"   they say and
scurry on down the shaolin passageways
the tunnels, or catacombs she lies in
stretch 105 mercury degree rising measure
quicksilver following break
cascading and soaring
could have reached 108
no one knows
faces,   fingers, reappear
pumping machinery
struggling writhing throughout stomach, throat,
eyebrows knitted, pursing lips
blood-drained pallor cheeks they
push and force
tug and pull away plastics
snapping eyes, heels part
fading far farther
white   the tunnels open wide
haunting dark red caverns tiny
obsidian chip eyes peeking through

the watchers   those without fear of man
I can only spectate as
she slips into   recall

dancers   on toe chaotic climax
extremities held in tight circles
bent elbow, dainty toes, black-gray claws
ears slicked back like
a scorned, angered mare
whiskers gleam, tails streaming along to
the dance   the dance
the Mardi Gras
the Coup d'état
the Marathon
They Shoot Horses Don't They?
their bodies wrapped in fur as if they
should be dressed, primped, combed
frenzy filled they   touch lightly   almost
a ballet, or tap, no, free
dance   they are free
from restraints
from being minor mammal
suddenly they huddle
gangly approach to center
like a sneak-up dance
exchanging excitement
they plan,   this is no instinct,
they prepare, premeditate
mutinous recapture of the den
those tunnels outside,   they
were not built by   hares   the
urine odor was not left by infants
dancers left this trace
to forewarn intruders

a single mother, newborn, and infant,
move in escaping her pistol-wielding spouse
lucky to be alive   she tells herself
paying the burly biker landlord
every   dollar she saved
for their escape,   battered, bruised,
splintered dreams,   she cradles both
babies climbing into the green
hand-painted slat board crib
nurses one gives a cracker
to the other

marching onto the so-called shelter
they appear through every
hole in ceiling, wall, and floor
a double dozen, or more,
they make their way into
the rooms   leaping with ease
their foot and foot and a half
from nose to tip of tail   lengths
lumbering onto shelves,
formica counters,   the one antique
dresser riddled with wormholes,
teeth gnaw continuously   turning
solid matter to Swiss cheese in the
den, the sheetmetal mobile home

the mother covers the sleeping
innocents   she clutches an empty   2-liter glass
Coke bottle in the right hand
and iron claw hammer with rough, splintered
wooden handle   in the left   she
tells the pack, the herd, the congregation
these are her children

she says this with her eyes
she wedges herself into the corner of the crib
staying guard through
weary length of night, she
swings on occasion when
one ventures close-range
hoping to take a finger as
the lost child from Birdtown lost toes
to these   years ago   gnawing, growing
teeth   in hopes of taking
the taste of milk
from sleeping baby lips
she connects at least twice each night
she never sleeps
the nightmares allow the rulers victory
dragging bones, her children's, from their teeth
like game trophies to be hung below floors
she dozes midday   in the
car with no gas and no floorboard
her babies tied to her
she never sets them down

"They are like tigers" her
dad told her "never corner them,
they become as panthers,
as Bengals" he told her long   ago
she wishes he had a
phone   or that she had one
to get a message to him
that he was right   that they
are here to prey on the
living, larger mammals   man
she remembers her mother's screams
at walls and stove ventilation

VISIT TEEPEE TOWN

raving conversation with tormentors
no one else could see
and leaving at thirteen
her brother pounding her face
with fists and pool balls
his favorite hobby
her father hard at work every day
as if he could work away the madness
her sister fleeing six weeks before
packing one suitcase as if it were an overnight
remembering the way she said
"when they dance, they have it"
she knows this true   firsthand,
she observes performance
the ritual
it terrifies her
the dance, the dance, bounding, leaping closer
here, she defends the trench of waller,
the foxhole crib they lie in
while the rulers plan strategies
and taunt her

amazed at their aggressiveness
she wishes for a gun,
or knife,   a better implement
to fight with during this
night they are especially
close   the light,   that one
single line,   precise between earth
and sky   both pitch
that clear blue white line appears
to break day,   crows caw
outside   the owls   make roosting sounds
the watchers chew and twitch before

jumping to floor, scattering
to holes and scampering out of light
into the ground   tunnels
into the underground
the den beneath this floor
like vampires retiring to mausoleums
to choreograph the "ring around the rosy"
for the new dusk to come
den of daytime
they sink into tunnels
like bats   in daylight
with the same ammonia-filled stench

the young mother
closes her eyelids momentarily
only to seal them slightly
the pull so taut
black rings below   she
slides over the crib railing
releasing bottle and club   no,
hammer   she thought it
a club   wish splitting manifestation
she changes babies and feeds
them   all she can
then bundles them
and ties them to herself
her sister once called her a pack-mule
babies cling like koala bear clip-ons
they know nothing of the danger
she raises them from
she wraps a big
towel around the three of them
covering her shoulders
with a faded car coat

they leave the
den   leave the lights on
repelling rodents
in their absence
they walk
the small mother
carrying the full
load of three
kicking stones
along the way
remembering days before
days of war on homefronts
racing from attacks
knowing that for her
there is nowhere safe to run
a single brown sedan
flies by them   on the long
stretch of highway
they amble alongside of
between steps they sigh
the gravel thickens
as they reach the country store
the wooden ramp under her feet
they enter

making way to shelving, hunting
hardware,   holding   careful watch
they locate traps
twelve inches long
she lifts four and then
four again,
lays eight on counter
she pleads for credit writing
promise on colored paper

the owner looks at her
at the traps
looks at her again
double-take
spine erect
she loads courage
in her eyes   agreement
reached, she raises the bag
he dropped them into
retrieving the items to count
eight   she works up a pressed
curve of lip into slight smile
they

return, armed
the babies know nothing   she thinks
and tells herself
she's doing all she
can to take care of them and at
least their father can't kill her   now
she is bigger than these dancers
these new adversaries   these
barons of the earth almost
as ancient as the roach   though
twice as evil
she imagines them
tremendous dragons
and plans masquerading carnival
invitational trap   once
again   inside the den
mobile home

the trailer is decorated in Early American cardboard
she never unpacked on seeing the rats

VISIT TEEPEE TOWN

the tiny woman gathers boxes,   these boxes
she sets in appropriate positions,
vantage points, they secure
at night she places scoops
of commod peanut butter and oil
on the traps' triggers and pulls
back the springs   tucking in
tongue catch,   setting force,   she lays
them ever so gently   deep inside
corrugated cubes
ripping newspaper
hoarded in her car trunk
to shreds
she gently, ever so
gently   lets the shreds and strips
fall   like crumbs of snow from her fingers
filling entirely the space above
the bottom, center-squared   sharply pulling
back her hands to let them
"lie in peace"
masquerading as nesting
materials   for those who come
at night   for their underworld
home   below her feet
and the crib's
legs

the sky outside casts
over   deepest gray, telltale coal
clouds surround the meadows   out
in the open
lightning time
begins
the strikes stab sky

Native Writings After the Detours

bolting toward the metal walls
and roof   she quickly places the
babies into high chairs   the chairs' legs
safely set into eight decaying
sneakers   four under each chair
the pots and pans
on the steel stove top
dance   from surges
untamed electricity
lights the burners
all four knobs read OFF
over orange-red coils bouncing cookware
the dead motor
in the air conditioner
buzzes, jars, and tries to turn over
though when she turned it ON
herself this strain never occurred
light bulbs   hanging exposed from the ceiling
glow brighter with each lightning stroke
charges ignite and leap at times from sockets
the rubber soles of old
shoes   protecting babies   barely
she has done this before
stranded during storms in previous escapes
her husband always found her
as if his sonar hits
were more direct than lightning
the baby caught in everything
then there was one, now there are two
the three a family
by blood and flesh
clap and crash   thunder pounds
sheet walls shimmy
vibrating from pressure and forces living, ruling

VISIT TEEPEE TOWN

eventually the rains join the streaks
and dance in electrical fallout
the drops and sparks   fire and
water

she sweeps the floor
watching the window   the black dung
pellets left overnight flying out the
doorway   day passes like all the
rest   this year   the dancers will
spin years of dreams   night terrors
dark cyclones filled with black eyes
scraping, gnawing, teeth   but
that is far into the future
she is here in the now
shadows skip sundial   night
falls as a shade
night shade
night watch
the dancers clamber
out of chambers onto the
porch   out of the sliding glass
doors   she carries the babies
to the bright green crib   and
lulls them to sleep
Indian songs she sings
she cradles them
in her arms until the slumber
is sufficient to last the night
time   she takes the bottle that
glass 2-liter   in her right
and the iron claw hammer
in her left and makes   ready
she catches the dancers bounding

so elegantly, so gracefully
she catches sight
and smell of the
dancers

they   watch her as
well   creeping closer together
they huddle tails entwined
they scheme, slink away,
file into formations
taking the walls,
floors and ceiling   by storm
combative stances
they laugh her off
through the night she connects
a few again   though they relish
their glory   as kings   she
nothing but a damsel
the largest dancer
a gift from Europeans
giant from Norway—the
King   he is a tyrant and always
taunting her   this time they
get bored   in this game and leap
showing off their egos inflated
they bound into boxes to
play with shredded stuffing and
quench the desire for
government-issue
peanut butter
        trigger snaps
tongue catch   and springs   f l y
sending steel   over
backs and   bones   and

fur   four times   then
rear lines   follow   four
more snaps   the others
have no heart for fallen fellows
and continue the taunting closeness
edging   toward   her babies
dodging glass and hammer   claw
the game so merrily played
throughout the hours in this
night   in the long
month of September   this
time she feels some sort of
security

when crack-light
dawn breaks the still sky
the survivors retreat   she
lifts the first box   the
rodent's dead weight
makes her sick
even though she
cannot see it through the
shredded papers   still filling
space   covering the body
weight and smell fill her
with fear that it will jump
toward her sight unseen
and lay its fangs into her
skin   she casts the box
at least twenty feet out
the door

she slowly walks
over to inspect its contents

the cadaver lies   back broken
twelve or more inches long
she wants to throw up but
has no time   all the others
sail out into the meadow
because each time she feels
their dead weight her arms
uncontrollably fling boxes
one by one until
eight are spread

hours later she recovers
the shock initial
and begins releasing traps to reset
peanut butter surprise
she washes her hands and
arms   for forty minutes
straight   before caring for
the children, for the day
the children know nothing, they're so
innocent, they don't know anything
it is so still, the wind drifting stench
is the only movement   the sky
remains dark, blackest black
gray-tipped lining cloud
boxes, traps, shreds,
boxes, traps, shreds
she commits to the order
front line in corrugated mine field
snap, spring, dancers fall
the flank moves forward

the landlord comes one day
when he arrives she cries   to

him begging for abatement
rent   on the den   he laughs
her off   his ears look like
the king's—pointed   she steals
serial number from his
work truck to garnish his
wages in court   she will sue
she says   he backhands
her   just as her husband did
so many times before   she
left him in June   paid the
rent three months' advance
to this wannabee slumlord
single dwelling dictator
this leech of land-
lord-ing   now the winter is
approaching fast   the babies notice
and cry they notice
they are aware
time is running   out

the owner of the store
is surprised to see her
he agrees to take her to town to file
small claims court   in a few weeks
the landlord tells the judge
that the reason the rats came
was because of her housekeeping

"No.   They were already here."
she says showing pictures of rats in
traps   she drew to scale
the babies crawl around the
courtroom   the people stare

and shake their heads   they judge,
they convict,   they send her to
jail   in their minds   "Your Honor,
it's the truth"   she says and he
allows her to reclaim one hundred dollars
suggesting she "look better
next time you rent" her shoulders
rise and tighten, lips part
salted words dissolve on her tongue
the babies scamper around
till they locate her legs
and climb
up to be held tight

a singer she knows tells her about
a basement apartment,
fixer-up rental they collapse
into   it smells sweet   they eat and
sleep   night passing   something
scratches and runs   in the
false ceiling   she sees black
eyes   in her mind   she hits
the white, dusty panels
and a possum falls
almost into her arms
she screams, then laughs hysterically
they get a cat, a real mouser
the feline patrols every night
protecting the babies
they sleep on a mattress
no longer in a crib
there are no shadows
from slats on their faces   babies
turn into tots and play

she writes songs
gathering random chords
prays to be left alone
and prays not to be lonesome
she falls to sleep writing and smiling
at her children

she dreams
she is in the tunnels of the
rulers   former terrorists   *who*
was the tenant?   this question
in dreamscape

her body becomes ridden with pain
sickness so strong
fever shoots so high
nothing can bring it down

five days have passed
amnesia, the sickness reels, she tries to cry
but her lips won't work
she lies in her own vomit
her hand reaches out with effort
to the silhouette of the younger child
she contacts dry parched skin like old
paper   paper-thin leather, fragile gray
her skin is also gray   she
can see it   the older child
across her feet both children out
cold   dying   or already gone
she cannot move
darkness, quiet silence, death is coming
she smells it and turns away
to turn,   to f a l l

to fall to the floor   she crawls
like the babies to the wall   she
cannot reach   the phone
she pushes open the door and falls

out into the cold
the fierce cold of this winter
her fever melts the snow next to
her gray, gray skin   schoolchildren
stumble across her body   and run
for help down the dirt road
they scurry
their mother lifts her into their
wagon   station wagon   they lay
her babies beside her in the back
Is this a hearse?
the clinic doctor will not
allow them within doors   "No way,
they are gray, look at them."
He covers his mouth and face with enormous hands
the strangers drive an hour to a
Public Health Service Hospital
and leave the three behind as they
hurry home for supper

the tiniest on saline intravenous
once he can speak
the biggest child tells the story
of the last five days
he fed the baby   while his mother
lay dying   "I thought she would
died" he says   explaining that after the third day
he couldn't feed the baby and crawled in with
her   he saw the baby crawl in the fourth day

"I think it was yesterday, dunno"
in another room she is told "They will make it,
you didn't lose your children."
"Can you hear us?"

the tunnels close
in around her the glass beads
black,   those eyes   like size
ten seed beads   glassy, shiny
they watch her, they rule

I

have witnessed all of this from
far   above   this
plague-ridden   room   floating
around   I feel free   enough to

dance

I

look back at she

once   I suppose   was me
too difficult   I decide
and watch a little longer   I slip in above
the babies
I know they need her to come back

delirious she yells "What's the cover routine?"
those hands slip a needle
to vein   she jerks   I jerk
with   her   and reclaim   the body

while the mind encounters steely eyes

dancers

plague dreams,   reality
leaping,   flying,   scampering
gnawing innocents
good healthy bodies
tearing away the escape of a lifetime
those tunnels   full to brim
rodents racing   through time
through this year   the fever

falls

chills rise my skin
bead goose bumps, my mind
is clearing   "Are the dancers gone?
Are the babies okeh?"   Hands and
faces embody nurses, doctors

"Have you had any recent contact
with any small animals?" they ask

recall dancers on toe   chaotic climax frenzy
they   dance   the dance   they dance

Percheron Nambe Morning

—for Travis and Vaughan and all the St. Catherine's Indian School kids

dust, leaves twirling
whirlpool
up off road
under wheels
undercarriage
automotive   winds
turning,   lifting
giving force to such
delicate   particles
ends attached in former
position to branch
soft paper thin petal-
like reds and golds
much as the mane swings
blows back   from higher
plane winds   Percheron   gold
mane   that red Percheron
on the right
the north side
you've seen her
in the early morning
when it's snowing she
raises her dignity
laughing at motorists
distressed by ice
and Pueblo patrol cars
we catch in peripheral
focus   signal   turn the
halogens off and on
on and off   until
they code the signal

distress signal
approaching tribal police
traffic trap
commuting   the
35 mph racket
through Nambe
Pojoaque turn   50
Tesuque Bingo/Pull-Tabs
long before the lodge
turned stone   near Camel Rock
before the Congested Area in
approach to the
"City of the Oldest Catholic Church in North America"
we convey these
danger signs   to
local yokels   perhaps even
tourists   if we're in mood
consideration
strange nation
neither of us belong
though   we do stay
in close   proximity to
these other   Native peoples
very different than where we
come from   still the same
only   *sometimes*   though
they know the patrol
man he's their cousin
all of theirs
they know this whirl
these leaves   rising now
before our heated grill
Chevy 4x   '91
they know the Percheron

she steals the scenery easily
with her laughter and turn
pitching hoof and tail
in mockery   indispensable humor
she takes this morning
under gray the shade of nickel
to cloud the stress enabling
me to speak to you of
beauty

Victoria Lena Manyarrows

The Language of Endangerment

the language of endangerment
means language that endangers
      language that defends
means language that stretches boundaries
& opens new doors.

the language of endangerment
are words from people under attack
      a world under attack
the earth, trees & sky endangered
by a selfish & money-driven culture . . .

we are the people who speak the words & language
      of endangerment
we speak words that endanger lies . . .

our hearts are open
our spirits are free
we speak
we speak
we listen & learn . . .

the language of endangerment pounds in our ears
        courses thru our blood
threatens us no more.

Besmilr Brigham

To the Unwritten Poems of Young Joy

I
that were.
that were not abstract as language is abstract
that did not demand description

from an animal age

the cry of the young wolf
the joy
of the wolf

a cat-joy sharpening its claws

not aware of sound, the joy of great waves
hitting the beach in storm
and the joy of unity

❀

i try to bring a unity to myself
to all the figures i am

VISIT TEEPEE TOWN

relationships

the human bonds that have broken the crystal
the learning that has torn
                                        like the wind in heavy
leaves, shattering their substance
emotion that is not pure

i would lie as a red leaf lies
fallen on the ground

                    ❀

the joy of the rock
that is past the joy of the shaping of the
rock

II
        joy is born in the heart
it is born in the seed, and past joy

there is observance

the cry of the old wolf
is a cry of knowledge

yet, in winter, how the old ones' cries at the breaks
of our pasture
can pierce the heart—

the old wolves coming deep from their safe lairs
to hunt, to kill, to ravage the herds of
sheep, cows in huddle, cows
their bellies full of the young
blood on the ground when the calves come, the wolves
crying
to get in to them

they smell the blood on the ground
the animal cries
are cries of terror

the written and unwritten poems past the point of
wonder
are poems of love
and poems of terror

that are
the structure of language

The Months Were Named For

time to plant corn
plaited mat, season to make reed mats in
the green tule
days of muddy ground, white
the first bloom

'soft and slippery' soil
second month of rain; and for
hatching

second arrival of baby birds

when sprouts grow, the moon of
wings—for all the feathered things
that fly
and Red Clouds (that come with late
storms) tangled mats

sun
of the crisp yellow stalks that wilt
first month, second

third—
of fields with flowers

and Chee Chee
when all the land
was happy with harvest
and big birds in the ripe corn
sang

the mask

how intently it looks down at me
holes for eyes
illusion against the wood, each

knife mark
hidden at last
in the natural curves of perspective, some
strange passing over of art

its countenance
still as my face lost in it, moves
when I move
the eyes interior follow

it is like a mirror, the man
carving from a tree cut
saw the mask; and the mask

saw. it sees now, its dedication
hung and controlled
what is the levy of pain? that draws
the human naked mind
hard to its suffering

laughter
an evil, negative joy

Bread and Wine: The old Bread and Wine Mission

—to Robert Duncan (in remembrance)

Hostel of the Mind—in darkness,
strangers
       sitting on old couch pillows on the
       floor together
in bonds of love, before the long high
table, high stool under a drop light;
light centered
we came together. a young man

reading, reading the Structures of
Rime. we see only the pages of a
mammoth manuscript, bound in words—
his hands moving the pages
of the script:
       the room is filled with
       echoes of his voice, a resonance
of purpose. Happy Warrior, loading his
Bow. out of the still night, a fresh

wash of rain, it comes to us: Song
of Language, melody of liberation;
feeling for blank spaces, i touch the
pen to paper, touching the flakes
of snow
that with sudden warmth melt, melt
in the hand, absorbent

crystals that enter the pores, shape
and reshape. Beauty is singular

she never runs in hordes. she is an
arrow held by a marksman, poison on
her tips (the poison of love)
    eternal as bread, the need for
sustenance. he has touched the shattered
ice; he is moving the avalanche: language,
in subtle rhythm
is absorbing the room, the walls, windows
that let out to a night out of

Holocaust; we are refugees, come to
benevolence. one of us has found the way
to the secret passage, tunneling like
a great furred mole . . . down under
where our secret ways are that have led
us to this place, to this point in time;
he holds up the lantern—
but this is his passage
    not ours, not to be shared
above the light there is darkness

And yet:
the vowel sounds glow. a phosphorous
in inky scrawls
glows on the pages; to be touched
    little bird feathers
    floating in light
    that i take to my shelter. Children

swept by the city into a place of seclusion;
we dance the Ronde of the dispossessed—
    hung like a star
    caught in a mesh of leaves
limb where the migrant lost hover
a cooling mist settles: in Circle of Sound

i move outward from the room. i have heard
the resonance of keys, the strung wires
of progressive and regressive tone, without
echo
clean as little bells hung in the light,
held in encompassing clarity:
    the Circle exists;
as Vowel creatures, we return to our lairs,
dungeons of the mind—
He is not the perpetrator. it will take a
life, under rain and stars, to find
now and then

the simple secret of the Fireglow, assonance
that in flight the minutest creature knows
an intoxicant Wine
that we mix with Bread

Heaved from Earth

after the tornado, a dead moccasin
nailed to the pole
boards scattered across a pasture

lying fierce crosses
jagged in mud

had flung itself
nail and wood
the square-head animal
hurled also in air

or as it raced in weeds
)water flowing, water falling
impaled
          both the snake and timber
went flying through with wind

coiled, made a coil (they do
immediately from danger or when hurt
and died in a coil
bit itself
in pain of its own defense the poison

                    birds
                    hurled into yard
                    fences
                    one with feet tangled gripping

             the open wire, a big Jay
struggling from the water
throwing its fanged head
high at the lightning, silent
in all that thunder

to die by its own mouth
pushing the fire thorns in

The Arctic Thaw

in the first days of the heavy north melt

no shadow, no vegetation

up and down the ice glades
a constant shower of bright crystal
the air is a hail of star ice
not heard,
north of the trees
snow left in moving tops the spear-shaft
pinewood
upright slabs fallen (in cliffs of flight

between the low cover, lost
the sun glassy
cold through a cut cold stands
like a shelf frosted and smokeless

shifting gales of fine as sand
swollen dunes
dust, source of the wind blown under
beating down over the still hooves of storm

       the body could only lie on its back
       the hands are folded over the nipples

a first huge fish
washed away from the early places
disappears in the rush under rock, a part
of sediment
naked between scattered clay the uncut
purity, fallen with stones

dead turf, limbs
quick spindling up bare in a marsh of water
cells in fluid stain moveable and
upright they pour
with the long withered and burned
glassed-over surfaces

on treeless oceans of ice

without context, image
monsters of the slide sheet and
rising thaw
submerge
a hard and sterile unity
on the effervescent

land
a wind-drive boat
pulls with the wind
under the full spray
melt
flinging long
    pulse heave-strokes
a wheel road
high among and washed to the stars

under the earth, women in earth

their tears

about the horizon, for night

the sun in lit large candles
molded from wax

vaulted in waving lines
clumsily built
clotted with animal blood

nearer, direct
riding over the low pass
a chapel with small bells
beating ornaments of bone and copper

that break in pieces from the scaled difference
quick in summer
pressed back sound, the motionless scabs of
thin white flakes

a melt-down from
        tumble bells of clover
surrounds the fields, glistening
goat horns hung silent on the walls
an infinity of fragments

                    the earth
                    abstract from heat
                    dreams singing with cold
                    impersonal
                    detached
                    isolate, the wings burn
in their steady lay cold

Nora Marks Dauenhauer and Richard Dauenhauer

Yéil Yaagú

—told by Jennie White

Kulixéitl'shan wé eey.
Daxdahéen L'uknax. ádi ax' héent wudzik' ít'.

Wé Ltu.aa yaa kawudaayí a tóodei wookooxú aa áwé.
Tlél tsú dleit káa yá Alasgi awuskú.
Tlé yú gus' yát wulihásh
at doogú daa.aaxw.
Tlé yá plástic gwéil ooyaa núch at naasí.
Xóots naasí.
Tlé dulxáash tsú áwé s wóochdei duskáa.
At naasí
gwéil áwé wé at doogú; tlé yú gus' yat wulihásh
   Ltu.aa.
Wé héench aan yéi kuwsineeyi át.
Ách áyá yá Alasgi kaadéi
Ánóoshi kuwashee.
Ayá a káx kuwduwashee yá Alasgi kax' Lingít.

Raven Boat

The rapids are very scary.
Twice the L'uknax̱.ádi capsized there.

This one boat traveled out of Lituya Bay
      when the tide had dropped.
No white man knew of Alaska.
The bundle of furs
floated out to the face of the clouds.
The intestines resembled a plastic bag.
Brown Bear intestines.
They are cut and sewn back together.
The intestinal
bag of furs floated to the face of the clouds
      from Lituya Bay,
the ones the people drowned with.
This is why
the Russians searched for Alaska.
That's how they found Tlingits in Alaska.

Has tsú tlél
tlél washéin has oo.oo, ch'a yéi
s'ís'aa een at has wulis'ées.
Ltu. aanáx̱ s'é kei aawlis'ís
Anóoshi yaagú.
Áwé
Lingít l atyax̱ sh koolneek.
Yéil yaagú áyú.
Yóo áyú kdunéek wooch een,
Yéil yaagú.
Yú Anóoshi áyú yéi yaa kanduník.
Wudusteení tle téix̱ yoo ḵugux̱sateek.
Ch'u yeedát yéi yatee yá Lingít.
Áwé yóot'át
s'áxt'.
A tóonáx̱ kukawduwatúl
ḵa
ketlháatl'i
gwéil yax̱ wduwaḵáa ḵa yátx'i náa
atoo yéi wduwa.oo.
Tléi téix̱ yoo ḵuguxsateek.
Yóo áwé Lingít aadéi yaa sh kagalnikch'i yé.
Wé s'íksh,
á ḵu.a áwé a toonáx̱ ḵukawduwatúl,
k´ei tunax̱kudutées' yáx̱.
A tóonáx̱ áwé dultínch
wé Ltu.aanáx̱ kei klas'ées.
Hél téix̱ ḵuguxsatee aagáa.
Ketlháatl'i tsú ḵaa séix̱ yawduwaḵáa.

They didn't
have machines either they'd just
sail with canvas.
A Russian boat
first sailed into Lituya Bay.
And so
the Tlingits didn't tell it like it really was.
It was the Raven boat,
was what they told one another,
the Raven boat.
That's what they were saying about the Russians.
If you looked directly at it you would turn to stone.
Even today the Tlingits are like that.
And that
devil's club.
They drilled holes in them
and
dog droppings
were sewn like bags
and put into their children's clothes.
You would turn to stone.
That's the way Tlingits talked about this.
This blue hellebore
was hollowed through though,
let's see, like binoculars.
As it sailed into Lituya Bay
they looked at it through these.
Then they wouldn't turn to stone.
Dog droppings too were hung around children's
        necks.

S'áxt'
ḵu.a áwé yéi kwdagei
tsú a toonáx̱ ḵukawduwatúl.
Ḵáa yátx'i
séi yei duwa. óo.
Aadéi yóo at kaawaniyi yé shukát
     wé shgóona shudultee nóok.

But the larger
devil's club
had holes drilled through them too.
They were put on the necks
of their children.
That's the way things happened in the beginning
    when they awaited the schooner.

Haa Shuka, *Our Ancestors: Tlingit Oral Narratives*. Recorded, transcribed, and translated by Fred White, and edited by Nora Marks Dauenhauer and Richard Dauenhauer. University of Washington Press, Seattle; and Sealaska Heritage Foundation, Juneau, 1987. PP 299 – 301.

The Woman Who Married the Bear

—told by Tom Peters (the Tlingit has been omitted in this story)

I

There were two women, sisters.
They went for meat
to the place where animals were killed,
the place where moose were killed.
When they were returning home
the meat was all
packed out.
That's when the two sisters
came on the berries,
they came on the berries.

Well, when they came on them, just then
the people left them behind.
Then the younger sister
said, "Hurry now," to her older sister.
She walked behind her.
She went quickly and
along where people had walked.

Then from there
the older sister
walked right through there
right through
right where
a brown bear
had defecated; she stepped on it.
That was what she slipped on, it's said.

And those berries of hers all spilled from her hands.
What was it she said then
to the Brown Bear? She insulted it.
But her sister had already left her.
That's when

that's when the man appeared in front of her.
Nice!
Where was this man from?
A young man.
As soon as he came by her he said to her
"Come with me,
come with me," he said to her.
"No!
My parents
will miss me."
"We will go there.
Just come, come with me forever,
come home with me,
come home with me
to the place where my home is."
At first she didn't want to go.
Maybe he did something to her mind.
Then she went with him.

They hadn't gone very far
when a log
was lying there.
They went over it.
They hadn't been going far
when another log was lying there.
They walked
for three days.
Here they were really mountains.
That's what seemed like logs to the woman.
Then, while they were walking along then
they came on people.
They were surely human beings; that's just how
            they seemed to her.
That's when
the one she had gone with said to her,
"Don't look up.
At dawn,
don't look among the people."
But then
at what point was it?
"I wonder why he's saying this to me," she thought.
Weren't they the woman's people?
Weren't they
her father
her mother?
"I wonder why he's saying this to me," she thought.
Then, when she woke up
at dawn
that's when

she pushed the blanket-like thing down from her face.
So many animals were asleep inside there,
brown bears.

From here
they separated from the people.
But from then on, the brown bear
        would hunt just around there.
There were salmon.
Things were drying
on the mountain—
ground squirrel
ground hog.

It was exactly
one year.
She had been gone with him
more than a year,
one spring and one winter.

When winter began coming
they had settled in.
She didn't know he was something else either,
        but thought he was a human being.
"We will live up there," he said.
How she liked it!
It seemed to her
like a house made of branches.
Nice!
It was very nice.

It was the way the house should be.
That's when
he told her
"Bring down some
branches
from up there for our bed."
The woman immediately went up there.
Then she knew what he was, that he was a brown
        bear who had captured her.
"Don't break the branches from up there.
Pick them from the ground."

Just then,
then when she broke the branches, she broke them
        from above.
Then she brought them.
"Let me see.
Did you break them from up there?
Yes.
Let me see!"
That's when she gave them to him.
"Drat!
I told you 'Pick them from the ground.'
Now you've marked where we live."

It was known
to her father
and to her mother
and others
where the den was.

They could see from her footprints that she had gone
with him.
Then they moved to a different place.
Then they stayed there, they stayed there.
She was with him long enough to have two children.
They were just
like people.
Then they moved to a different place.
They settled there.
How the people of our village are
that's how they were.
Everything,
there was nothing that they needed,
at home.

But that time
there were five of them
the brothers of hers.
That was when they tried.
They could see their sister's footprints; they
        could see
that she had gone
with that thing.
He knew immediately that his life
        was in their hands.
When spring returned, when spring finally returned,
the brothers of hers
all five of them,
picked medicine leaves.

They did it just to get him,
just to get the bear.
It is truly sensitive
people say.
Do you know what is called "leaves?"
That's the first Tlingit you didn't know.
(N.D.) Is it made to acquire something?
Yeah! Yeah!
It is known here that they were imported from
            over there.
This was told to us.
I never wanted to try those things.
It is really strictly handled, they say.
They are the ones,
they are the ones
that were made for things like money.
And these too were made correctly.
Maybe it was something that made you crazy, they say.
They made medicine,
from then on, medicine was made.
Eight days,
for eight days
in the morning
no
food was eaten
and no water,
water,
no water was drunk.
Then spring really returned,
spring time
April.

Now they tried.
Then there used to be
dogs
trained with medicine.
"Chewing Ribs"
was the name
of the dog.
Those brothers
didn't go searching just once.
Today
this morning
the eldest
would go
to the hill.
Then the next one
then the next one.
Ah, ha!
At one point it was the turn of the youngest
of the woman's brothers.
When spring
returned
she would go outside, groping her way, like this.
Ah, ha!
Spring finally returned.

That's when
the animal,
the brown bear,
had a vision
of his brothers-in-law.

"Your brothers
are making medicine against me.
Oh, oh.
Oh, oh.
It seems like it's the youngest who will get me.
Be brave."
That's what he told her, what the one with her
told the woman
and her children too,
both of them.
"Be brave.
When I fall into their hands, be brave,
when I fall into your brothers' hands."
At that time the woman would beg the animal
        with all she could.
"Have pity on my brothers.
don't do anything to them,"
she would say to it.
"The younger one,
your younger brother will be the one."
From then
he already knew what the woman
was going to do.
There were two
stones this size.
Each time they ate
she'd roll them secretly
in his food.

When she finished doing that,
"There!
But it seemed to him as if she had done it
      openly.
Surely the bear was an animal of the forest.
"There he is!
Your brother is coming here.
Be brave."
Just as soon,
as soon as it became dawn
his thoughts shot in,
his thoughts.
Here,
when they shot inside
they were just like a beam of light,
maybe they were just like a flashlight.
That is how they shot
through the house.
He caught the beams right there.
He snapped them back outside.
These were people's thoughts, it's said.
Because of that the black bear
and the brown bear
can see people.
They're pretty hard to find.
That's why he couldn't find it,
why he couldn't find the den,
because of his thoughts.

When a man's thoughts
are shot inside its den,
he snaps them back toward the entrance.
That's why they can't find it.
Heh.
Ah, ha.

When she heard this from him,
when he told her those things,
that's when
the woman finally went out to the entrance of
         the den.
Here
she put those stones
between her legs,
those stones
she had,
then, toward the beach,
on the side of the mountain,
on the frozen
crust
she rolled them down,
those things rolled down
and he found one.

He walked along the side of the mountain.

That dog of his
knew right then,
that dog of his that hunted with him.
Heh!

While it was going along
it acted
as if it got a scent of something in the snow.
It ran around sniffing.
Here it was where the stone had rolled down,
          wasn't it?
Up that way
he followed it.
The people of today
are not like the ones of long ago.
They were tough.
If they went from here no matter
          how many miles they had to go
          they'd make it in a day.
And now . . .
What are they?
"Ah hah!
Ah, ha! your brother's getting close,"
he told her, it is said.
Then like when
spears
are hung from rafters
is how his teeth looked to the woman.
He pulled them out
from there.
That is when she really
begged of him,
"Pity my brother," she said.

He was approaching up there.
Heh.
Then
suddenly the bear heard the dog barking
from the topside.
It wasn't like a dog of today
They were as smart as humans
long ago.
Well, probably they were the same on the coast, too,
those dogs.

Over there
it is always done like this when the entrance
        of a den was approached.
From the upper side.
You can't go straight up.
Only from the upper side.
Whatever, even a piece of clothing, was tossed in.
That is what he did.
He tossed his mitten
into the entrance.
He could only see the paw
inside
then sweeping behind.

"Be brave,
I will go out
to him.
I will play with your brother,"
he said to her, it's said.

The bear lured him
into coming down.
That's when he instructed her.
"When your brother finishes with me
don't be careless with my skin.
You tell them right away.
You tell him.
Drape my skin
with the head
toward the setting sun."
That's why it's still done now.
From this very story.
It is never tossed away carelessly.
A pole is placed under it thus.
It is hung and pointed
toward the sunset,
from his words.

He came right to the entrance there.
He stood facing it.
Ah ha!
But even at that
his dog didn't tire from barking.
He had already killed the bear.
He went up to it.
What else was there in the den?
Someone spoke from inside.

"Your mouth will get tired,
Chewing Ribs?"

He just stood there.
What's more, his sister came out of there,
the one who had been gone
so long.
He got her.
The children also,
the two of them.
"From there
this skin of mine
you will always keep with you,"
is what he had said to her.
That's when he taught her
this song of his.
"You will sing this
when you hang my skin,"
he said to her.

(At this point, Tom Peters sings two songs.)

II
It was
the brown bear
that I was telling about.
Then
things were settled.
She became accustomed to her village people.
Then
she lived the way

she had as long ago.
It was then she had her husband's
former skin
the way he had told her to do.
Yes. "When you go out
you will put this skin of mine
on your back."
Yes; this is what he once told her.
From then her children
had reached her size.
Then
she would leave them
when people would hunt ground squirrels.
She would only go a short way.
How did she get the squirrels?
Only the mound of her pack would be seen
          moving along to her house.
Only when she was ready to go
would she pull on
the skin that was her husband's.
Yes.
At times it would be going after berries,
when she was going to get berries.
Just as she was leaving home, as she started
          out, she would pull it on.
She would become
a real bear.
Her children too.
Up there where last year's berries grew
in the berry patch.

She would come out on the mountain.
Her children with her too.

After doing this so many times,
the brothers of hers
asked their mother
"Mother!
will you tell my sister
we want to just play a game with her?"
That was when she told her mother
"No!
No!
It is not right
for them to do this to me.
Yes. I am not the same anymore as I used to be.
When
I pull on
my husband's
skin
I don't think my old thoughts anymore.
This is why. No!
Let me be.
Let me live among you for as long as possible."
But still the brothers asked her
"Mother! please ask
our sister
to let us play with her."
How many times
they must have asked this.
Finally she said to them
"Well, okay, let's go!"

Let's go!
Let them play with me."
After she said this to her mother
she left.
As soon as she left home she pulled on
the skin of her husband.
She looked just like a brown bear.
Her children too
the two of them
went alongside of her.
It was up there
above everyone on the face of the mountian
among the berries.
This is when she came out there.
Maybe they didn't believe shc would.
The blades
of the arrows
were
pieces of bark.
Pieces of bark were placed on the tip.

Except the blade of the one who found her,
her brother, the youngest one.
It was he,
there were two arrows of his.
They each had
u real arrowhead.
There was
what is called
a quiver.

Arrows
are kept inside it.
It's worn around the neck.
He put the arrows inside it.
He didn't do to his sister what his
            older brothers did, it's said.
He only watched.
From then his older brothers
stalked her.
The way an animal
is struck with arrows
is how they did it.
When the first one's arrow,
when the first one's arrow
struck her
was when her cry was heard.
"From behind you."
Here's when she turned on them.
How many of them were there? They were helpless
            against her.
And her children too.
When they were dead is when the younger brother,
the one with the two arrowheads,
drew them out.
            (Slap!
            Slap!)
He killed her,
that sister of his.
Now that is the end.

Diane Glancy

Tomatos

A string of tamoots \
break into them \ spurt
green sleeds \ gerzy.
A tribe of matoots.
Constellations \ their scattered feathers.
Look into the black space of buffalo.
Language neighs in the krummholz
& static electricity gerps the prairie
with afterburn.
Warriors once more squecching their war whoops
slide down the cords of lightning
back to dance in prairie ooze \
ototams tied to their loins.
They slip through when the wind is up.
Winter magnatism. Matotos.
Umbrageous woods of space \
a string of fish hangs from their braids.
I think they prefer the prairie
to the south coast of the stars.
Red skinned \ ottomas.

EEE AY WHO TWO

Eee ay who two
_____

stony ground	the stars at night
starry sky	white stones in the field
I hear the markings now	
hoe tow	hoe tow

Hosanna   annasoh
_____

backward over trails	nowhere
forward now	
they give the bible	spilling rain

Tom bey
_____

rusted mailbox in the yard	
arsenal of distance	ansonal
stout blue soldier	stripped of his coat
we pot	shot him

Sohanna   nasohna
_____

here	they say
turkey barns in these hills	counterfeit arks.

Death Cry for the Language

GRANDMOTHER

tuya:taht'a'	*branches at the top*
ti:yawhi:t.la	*land lizard*
huni:kawheh'	*they saw*
ah:kwahi:'	*big*
i:kit'a	*size*
atsilaha	*all afire*
diti:k'a'nheh'	*he was looking at us*
na'yaha'	*all rocks*
awtali'	*over big mountains*

HER DAUGHTER

On that cold morning in the boarding school
they lined up the language to be shot
the air was hard against us
we heard the guns
watched the words fall
there was no-light from the sun.

THE GRANDDAUGHTER

I lived on the edge of town NEARLY A YEAR
TWICE the wind touched down
ripped husks from corn
roof from a house & shed
Sometimes the wind is GRAVITY
I feel it lift when I walk down the road
Other times of course
it's got a hand like my Father

but IT'S THE ROCKS that hold the house down
the way memory HOLDS—
so that NOT ANYTHING
the green sky gives can matter.

GRANDMOTHER
Grandpa & Grandma left Georgia in the old country, some came
from North Carolina, the old country too. Mamma was a girl then.
The Soldiers drove um out. They didn't want to come. Soldiers said
go or they'd kill. They'd stick bayonets in um. Some got pots, dishes,
skillet, clothes, yuh, bed clothes too. I've got the dish Grandma
brought. I eat beans out um. But some came with nothing, not
shoes, not blanket. Next day Soldiers drove um west. 1st day easy.
Grandma said Soldiers felt good. But every day got worse. Just drove
um like cattle. Grandma said she walked in snow, Grandpa walked
too. They crossed creeks to chins, lots of mud. Crossed rivers on
rafts, hollow logs. Soldiers had wagons. Fed um 2 times some days,
sometimes feed 1. Soldiers ate all the time & took care of horses.
Lots of Cherokees were sick & died, too weak to walk. They buried
um beside the trail. Clothes got bad, shoes too. Most clothes all gone
when they got to new country. They found lots of trees but the land
was no good in hills. The good land awtali' was over the mountains
in old country. Grandma hated the Trail of Tears to tuya:taht'a'
Indian Territory.

HER DAUGHTER
Co-To-Te in his Father's Packard with the deer antlers on the hood.
A zigzag border on the lap robe. Half his face painted red, his hack-
led tail, he STRUTS—TOM TOM TOM TOM. HEY EY EY EY. The wood-
land singers POW WOW DRUMS. The sky's face painted half-green.

Some of them came to land with oil sleeping under it. Ho HA! The oil rights buy them shiny beads.

THE GRANDDAUGHTER
Grandma had a scar on her face.
ATSI:LAHA was her old name (all afire).
Her braids crawled in the cookfire
& the FLAMES climbed to her face.
Sometimes in the wind
I smelled her burnt hair & flesh.
She kept a small Rock under her bed
her Grandpa carried from Georgia.

GRANDMOTHER
N' YU' NUWI (stone coat-on)
I have a small Rock my Grandpa brought from Old Territory.
It's from STONE COAT. Long ago, he lived among our people.
He was a wicked CANNIBAL covered with scaly armor. He went from place to place where people did not suspect him. Sometimes he was invisible—killing um for his food. If he came he killed & ate everyone & there was ONLY 1 way to save the people—He COULD NOT look on menstrual women—If they found 7 to stand in his way the sight would kill him. So the Medicine STONE COAT came. Soon they heard NA' YU' NUWI through the woods. He came along the trail where the 1st woman stood & soon he saw her he said Yu! grandchild in BAD state! He hurried past but soon came to the next & cried again Yu! my child in terrible way! He hurried past her but now he VOMITED blood. He met the 3rd & 4th & 5th & 6th woman each one his step grew weaker until when he came to the last from whom sickness had just begun—NOW BLOOD poured from his

mouth & he just FELL on the trail. Then the Medicine Man drove 7
stakes in his body & pinned him to the ground. When night came
they piled logs over him & set him on fire to him & all the people
gathered. NA′ YU′ NUWI was AD′WE-HI Holy Man & told MEDICINE
SONGS for Healing. At midnight he sang the Hunting Songs for
calling bear & deer & turkey & animals of the woods & mountains.
As the blaze grew hotter the voice of NA′YU′NUWI sank lower until
by daylight the logs were a heap of white ashes & his voice was still.
Then the Medicine Man raked off the ashes & there was red WA′DI
paint for face for hunting & U′LUNSUT′I (magic stones)!

HER DAUGHTER

It was easier for the women I guess. There was always supper to get
on the table. The men were the ones wiped out. They didn't know
what to do. The new land couldn't be farmed. They lost their Spirit.
Their will to plow & raise animals. When there's nothing to do you
lose yourself in drink. My mother's 1st husband was dead before he
died. He left her with several small children to raise. All the talk
about the Spirit & I never knew what it was. The men came around.
They lived off her for a while. We always got supper to get on the
table.

THE GRANDDAUGHTER

I take the Rocks with me
no matter where I live.
I think 1 year I lived 5 different places.
I move in & get my Rocks settled
then I feel the Spirit move on & I follow.
Or I move in with someone & it doesn't work out.
1 house I lived in

I knew something bad had happened on the land.
Whoever helps me move
(though I can do it myself)
says what's that box of Rocks?
Now sometimes I put them in other boxes
so one is not so heavy & put a blanket on top.

GRANDMOTHER
ye ye in old beaver-hunting ceremony
Dancers circle with shuffling step
they carry a stick on their shoulder like a gun
DAWN:HI:LI (going to hit with something)
they hold the stick in their left hand
strike dead beaver in the circle
Dancers cry HYU HYU
the beaver JERKS when Dancers strike
TAWY TAWYI YO:HYO! Stone Coat Hunting Song.

HER DAUGHTER
Well, he cleared his throat
a fat-bellied man in high-heeled boots
his pony tail down his back
I'm Co-To-Te's son (cough)
I went to a pow wow last year
& everything went wrong
(step back, look away)
A man died—maybe a heart attack or the heat
Then a car caught fire & burned
just like a house
2 tribes got in a fight (cough)

(song about pow wow)
I was in prison
(step back look away)
not much difference (cough)
from boarding school
(people laugh)
only they don't kill you as fast
in the school (clear throat)
(people laugh)
I'm on my way if I can make it
somewhere in Kentucky (cough)
they're digging up burial grounds
stealing face masks
(step back, look away)
if you know the spirits you know
you can't disturb the dead
(step back, cough, look away)
or you & your family are in danger
We're going to sing songs about the digging up
(cough, look away)
I got 25 years to serve in Ohio
(sing prison song)
the priest said peace on you
a little boy who could hardly talk
said peece on you father
(people laugh)
I can't tell the other jokes I know
(sing about love)
I think I'm in love yeah yeah yeah

THE GRANDDAUGHTER

Most people don't believe in animal transformaions anymore, but
the other night, I, the OWL—HOOTED IN THE OAK—WHO WHO WHO
HI:YATSITU'HI:HI:YO. The night was full of bugs, flying spirits,
really, I sat in the tree—I heard Grandmother talk—She spoke so
softly I could hardly hear her. It was as though IF I turned her up,
I'd hear there was NOTHING there. That's the terrible secret I have
to keep—WHO WHO WHO!!!

GRANDMOTHER

I whisper because it's wrong to speak
My throat-hurt from swallowing words.
my neck swell as if I wear goiter tuya:taht'a'
        ti:yawhi:t.la
        huni:kawheh'
        ah:kwahi:'
        atsi:laha
        diti:k'a'ɪɪheh'
        ha'yaha'
        awtali'
Our land back east over Rocky Mountains.
But lizard took it & marched us to woods of Indian Territory.
We had vision of big fire. They said it is army marching through
our old lands.

HER DAUGHTER

The QuiVerEE. ZEET! ZEET! The little clawed feet of the turkeys
DANZE I Mourn for Co-To-Te. The Warriors we lost. The land that
sank with THEM. When you take a man's language, you take his
meaning. Acht! That's the bang of it at sunrise. The firing squad

of light. The quibble-ree. Your words rush out of you like dust from a mop in the prairie wind. You see yourself fly—Blown far way without a chance of getting back, no matter what. The truth is— without words, you're a ghost of yourself hanging on.

THE GRANDDAUGHTER
I count my rocks everyday.
That one with Spirit coming out—
The other black as night
(It was CoaL from kenTucky).
I have a Rock with a white line
        falling like a comet.
A smooth Stone from the tongue of a creek.
SpoTTed Rock. RockET.
Fozzil ROck.
RocK with the swirl of a wind-cloud
that touched down TWICE while I lived in that house—
But the Rocks held the floor down.
NOW I Dance in my leg-rattles around the fire.
WHO WHOOOOOOOO!!
Moon RoCk like my Grandmother's scar.
Sometimes I hold a rock & think I hear voices.

GRANDMOTHER
In the Boarding School for Indian girls, the oil lantern was a campfire on the table at night. Shadows flickered the wall where animals prowled. Some girls died with smallpox. Others screamed when they saw their faces. At night I felt the old burn on my cheek & sang the Medicine Song. I watched the Ancestors rise in half-sleep—Warriors strutting across the pitted face of the moon—

HER DAUGHTER

The moon slants back into the corridor of that old boarding school.
I could believe in transfer again—standing in line for vaccination,
my legs quivering like a rabbit's. The slick floors & bare walls.
Nothing to hold on to but air. My mouth tasted coppery. We all
cried. Afterwards the hard wind blew all night—Windows clucked
like hens. Soon I saw the 1st round black moon high on my arm.
Later the paler one under it.

THE GRANDDAUGHTER

I'd sneak out the window at night.
The screen was torn anyway.
They knew I was gone.
Hitchhike into town with anyone who passed.
I marked my year with drunkenness & arrest.
I had a friend—
sometimes we—
well, she knew a man
a veteran in a wheelchair
with an American flag over his lap.
We'd dance for him without our clothes.
He'd howl old hunting songs   HYU HYU
& we let him—
Well—he could make us—
with—

GRANDMOTHER

Acht. He sat in the boarding school & watched us like a lizard.
diti:k'a'nheh. If we said 1 word in Cherokee we had to chew a bitter
leaf. It made some vomit. But at night in sleep, Ancestors rubbed
our stomachs, gave us old food of our Langauge.

HER DAUGHTER

We came to Indian Territory 3 generations ago—my Great-grandma & Great-grandpa—My Grandma was a girl when she came. HEY EY EY EY. Where are the noises our Grandfathers made?

THE GRANDDAUGHTER

I loved a boy too. But my Mother didn't like him. She sat on the porch when he came to our house & scratched her crotch. But I went with him. Then he married someone esle. But I could't settle on anything then, slept with his friends. Once he wrapped the label from the neck of a whiskey bottle around my toes. The girls would talk about—the back seat of a car, the creek—what else did we have to talk about—the history of our territory as a concept of the mind?

GRANDMOTHER

ta'su'yah	*(we are) scratching spreading leaves*
ta'su'yah	
ta'su'yah	
ta'su'yah	
tak tak	*(turkey voice)*
tak tak tak	
tak'lu	*(turkey gobble)*
tak'lu	

In the woods the Grandfathers hide under a thick mat of moss. They cut eyeholes in their cover & fasten chestnut leaves for ears of the wildcat. Under moss, the Grandfathers wear woodchuck masks with deer-tails for ear-tufts. They crawl along the ground with magic of the wildcat, nearing turkey where they hide. The Grandfathers blow their leg-bone-of-the-bird whistle. ta'su'yah tak tak. They are mighty hunters of turkeys where they hide.

VISIT TEEPEE TOWN

HER DAUGHTER

Co-To-Te was mutilated with 2 other Indians on State Road 3. I
knew somewhere, far way, he took a white-face mask, danced in the
backyard of space. red rings around his eyes—A rooster jerking his
comb & wattle. He sweeps the stubbled dirt. Nearby a boy drums
his head with a stick, opening hs mouth for hollow sounds. Now a
girl pulls her arms into her sleeves. Co-To-Te spills black pocketsfull
of seed for them. The side-dancers chant to ho to ho. Co-To-Te
taps his clawed feet. The children gather the seeds for the green &
half-red earth in their heads somewhere.

THE GRANDDAUGHTER

4 generations ago we came to the New Territory which was later
Oklahoma. My Great-great-grandma & Great-great-grandpa.
Great-grandma was a girl when we she came. Now I am left with
hollow words which have no meaning. Hi′yatsitu′hi·hi·′yo.
Rifle-barrel
whiskey-bottle
closed-off throat—
the narrow passages from this world.

Mother of Mosquitos

CHARACTERS
Mosquito
Woman
Chorus
Forest

SETTING
Village of Ice in the Far North of the Imagination

Acknowledgment to the Eskimo belief that driftwood comes from an underwater forest

MOSQUITO
EEEEEEeeeeeeeeeee.

WOMAN
Swat.
Why mosquito fly near us?

CHORUS
She drinks blood.
Her life's in our blood.
Red drops come to our arm like leaves.

WOMAN
What's leaves?

CHORUS
Little mosquito-bumps on trees.

WOMAN
Where trees?

VISIT TEEPEE TOWN

CHORUS
> In the underwater forest
> where the driftwood comes from.

MOSQUITO
> EEEEEEEEEEEEEEEeeeeeeeeeeeeeeeee.

CHORUS
> Her story get into ear.

WOMAN
> Swat.
> I go underwater.
> No mosquito there.
> I step into fish-mask.

CHORUS
> Step.

WOMAN
> I become one with the mask.
> Sweet mask.
> No childbirth pains.
> No tattooing-needle in my face.
> No soot-black thread drawn through my cheeks.
> I wear fish-mask now with a huge lower-lip.
> I jump into ice-hole.
> Blub. Blub.
> My fins move like waves.

CHORUS
No mosquito bites her now.

WOMAN
But fish-spear whizz by to spear fish.
Whew. Enough.
I'm tired of wearing fish-mask.
I'm going back to shore.

MOSQUITO
EEEeeee.

WOMAN
Light the blubber-grease fire.
Smoke keeps the mosquito away.

CHORUS
No.
Make a fire from driftwood.
We tired of blubber-fire.
We tired of blubber.

WOMAN
I look for driftwood.
Where? Where?
There's no wood on the ice.

CHORUS

Under the ice is the water.
Under the water is a forest
where driftwood comes from.

WOMAN

I didn't see a forest underwater.

CHORUS

It's where our dreams go when we sleep.

WOMAN

Wrap me in the seal-skin tunic.
I sleep-walk to the ice-hole. I carry my dreams.
Glub. Glub.
I swim like a seal underwater.
Move out of way, fish!

CHORUS

Our voices call the driftwood—Hey driftwood.
We underwater-swim.

WOMAN

Feel the water-currents.

FOREST

That's underwater wind.

WOMAN

I look for driftwood to keep mosquito away.
Look. Look.
Can't find.
Where's the underwater forest?

FOREST

Who says there's a forest?

CHORUS

Our stories say.

WOMAN

The chorus say get wood. Get Wood.
All day.
But I don't know how to get.

FOREST

You hear stories of the underwater forest
where driftwood comes from?

CHORUS

Our stories say.

WOMAN

What are these seal-lure sinkers
jumping at my head?

FOREST

Those are leaves.

WOMAN

What's leaves?

FOREST

Leaves are the little teeth of trees.
First they're green as light in underwater sea.
Then leaves turn yellow as evening-sun.
Some leaves turn red as seal-blood on ice.

WOMAN

The trees change masks?

CHORUS

How we get this story straight?

FOREST

Then leaves go away.

CHORUS

Oh.
Where go?

FOREST

Like old ones to their death—
The women onto the ice.
The old men to a hunting land.

CHORUS

They go-away.

FOREST

Sometimes the tree goes away too.
Maybe even some of it
when driftwood floats to the surface
and waves carry it to the ice.

CHORUS

The leaves are little waves.
They come back and back.
They are given to us like stories.
We know things now.
These dreams are our masks.

WOMAN

I dream-dance in a seal-skin tunic.

MOSQUITO

EEEEEEeEEEEEE.

CHORUS

Swat.
Cannot get away from mosquito.
Even in dreams.

WOMAN

Make whale to blow mosquito through his air-hole.
Make tiny tiny spears to find mosquito-heart.

CHORUS

Up. Up. To the village of ice.
She wakes now.
She swims like a seal.

WOMAN

Swim. Swim.
But where's ice-hole? Cannot breathe.

MOSQUITO

EEEEEEEEEEeEEEEEEEEEEeEEEEEEEEEEe.

CHORUS

Here's the ice-hole!
Mother mosquito fly above.
Look at her big as an igloo.

MOSQUITO

EEEEeeeeeeeee.

CHORUS

Follow her sound.

WOMAN

Swim. Swim.
Now I back without driftwood from underwater forest.

CHORUS

We order driftwood now from catalogue.
Let the fire sing like a yellow-leafed tree.

MOSQUITO

    EEEEeeeeeeee.

WOMAN

    Let the red leaves remember our blood
    the mosquito sings us to the surface for.

CHORUS

    The mosquito brought us from the underwater-world.
    She heard our dreams cry from the underwater forest.

MOSQUITO

    EEEEEEeeee.

WOMAN

    You big mosquito. You mother mosquito.
    Show us your little spear-tooth.
    Bite. Bite.
    You bring us to the air.
    Your life is in our blood.

Phil Young

Performance at Cherokee Trading Post (I-40, W. OK.)

Untitled (Red Man Chewing Tobacco)

I Cannot Speak (But I Can Write Jeep Cherokee)

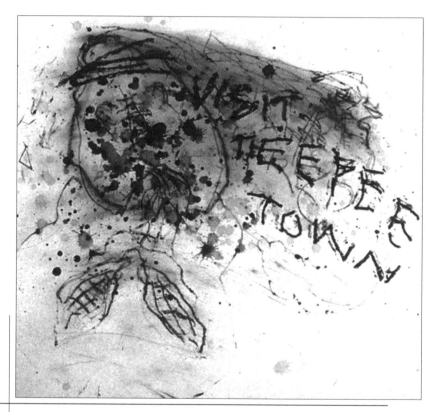

Visit Teepee Town

Larry Evers and Felipe Molina

Coyotes in "Ringo Bwiapo": On the Return of the Yaqui Song Tradition

April 11, 1987, on the eve of Palm Sunday, with an Easter moon on the rise, the Coyotes came back to Old Pascua. And with them came a traditional genre of poetic expression that has not been performed in that Yaqui Indian community since 1941.

We write to tell a part of the story of that return and to offer transcriptions and translations of the nine songs to which the Coyotes danced the night they came back.

Victor Lucero, Timothy Cruz, Steven Garcia, Felipe Garcia, and Joaquin Garcia were the Coyotes who danced that night. Felipe S. Molina sang for them. Their performance was the culmination of a long period of preparation. Felipe Molina remembers the events that led to that performance this way:

> About 1982 Larry Evers gave me a copy of some Coyote songs that Amos Taub had collected from Yaqui elders, such as Ignacio Alvarez and Refugio Savala, in the Tucson area in the early 1950s. This collection provided me with new songs that I could learn to sing. I went ahead and practiced the songs for my own interest, but as I practiced I was keeping in mind that maybe one day I would sing for some Bow Leader dancers.

It so happens that in my village the young boys, ranging in ages from, let's say, six to about eighteen, are interested in doing various forms of Yaqui dance and song. Some of the boys have learned many deer songs. They all have performed in a village or household *pahko*. Some have also learned some of the steps and movements of the deer dance. Because I have been working with these boys, I have been noticed in the Yaqui communities around Tucson. That is how Raul Cancio came into the picture.

For many months Raul Cancio tried to get in touch with me to talk about the Bow Leaders. I always forgot to call him back or to leave a message for him. Victor Lucero is one of the boys that I sing with in the village. Victor pushed me along the way to get a Bow Leader group formed. He was the person that kept telling me that Raul Cancio wanted to talk to me about forming a Bow Leaders group. I didn't give much thought to the idea then but it always stayed somewhere in my mind.

So finally in the fall of 1985 I met Raul Cancio for the first time, and we talked awhile about ourselves. He knew something about me, but he was a complete stranger to me. However, I knew his wife because she was a godmother to my nephew. Anyway, from this conversation developed the notion that we would start a Bow Leader group and that Raul would provide the necessary headdresses and other regalia if I would sing. We decided to hold the practice sessions in Yoem Pueblo at my house. So through this meeting our friendship was made and a Bow Leaders group was formed at Yoem Pueblo.

I did not intend to be in Old Pascua at all during the Holy Week ceremonials in 1987. I had intended to go to Potam in the Rio Yaqui area, so that I could see the Looria there. But I was given a godchild to sponsor for Holy Saturday in Old Pascua, so I could not go. So with that responsibility I had to stay for Holy Saturday. Since I was going to be there I was asked to sing for the deer dancer during the Palm Sunday pahko and also again to sing for him during the Looria and the Holy Saturday pahko.

Before Lent, Victor Lucero kept asking me if the new Bow Leaders group could participate in the Easter ceremonies. I said I didn't really know because I thought I might go to Potam. So we never got started at the beginning of Lent. So finally Palm Saturday was approaching so

Victor got on my case again and wanted to know if the group could dance at the pahko. I told him that I really couldn't tell him yes or no because I was going to be singing for the deer dancer. He said I could alternate between the Bow Leaders and the Deer. Finally through much contemplation I agreed and told him I would talk to the Fariseo Captain. The Captain was delighted to hear the request. He said *heewi*, it would be wonderful. So it seems that the group, especially Victor, was very happy to participate in the ceremonials. The group all went and danced and participated in the pahko. I alternated between the two groups all night long, first singing the Deer Songs inside the rama with the raspers, then going outside with the drum to sing Coyote Songs. Yaqui people were very happy to see and hear the two groups. The non-Yaquis who came seemed very happy, too, but most of them did not know what we were doing. They thought that the Bow Leaders were part of the deer dance.

I am grateful to Victor for his determination. He convinced me to accept his suggestion.

Wo'im, Coyotes, is what most Yaquis call them now. But in the talk of Yaqui elders they are appropriately called *Wiko'i Yau'ura*, the Bow Leaders. The Bow Leaders have served Yaqui communities for centuries as a military society. They are mentioned in the writing of a Jesuit missionary who worked among the Yaquis. Two and one-half centuries later, the Bow Leaders remain active in many of the towns along the Rio Yaqui on the wide coastal plain south of Guaymas, Sonora: Torim, Vikam, Potam, Rahum, Pitahaya, Loma Vahkom.

As recently as 1927, the Coyotes took up their bows and arrows and their rifles against Mexicans who were attempting yet again to appropriate Yaqui lands. Today they are most visible during certain pahkom, ceremonial occasions when Yaquis gather to perform religious rituals and to celebrate. On these occasions the Coyotes dance and perform burlesques to special songs, as they work to entertain those drawn to their performances. What they do with their songs and their dances is playful, light-hearted, fun. But their dance and song contribute, too, to their most fundamental role and their most serious duty: the Bow Leaders are the stewards of *Hiakim,* the Yaqui homeland, and they are bound by sacred vows to protect it.

The main function of a Bow Leader was to protect the land for the people. Nowadays the society's main function is a religious duty. The Bow Leaders have many obligations to the church and other ceremonial activities throughout the year. At the same time they act like guardians during a ceremonial to keep drinking and fighting out of the plaza or the household patio where a ceremonial is taking place.

Before the person decides to become a lifetime member he or she goes through many hours of counsel to get a better view of how it is to be a member. Many sad stories are told about how hard it can be during certain ceremonies when there is no food, when the weather is too cold or too hot, or when fatigue makes carrying out the duty very difficult. Stories are told that death is probable in times of war and that the one who is initiated could become food for the wild animals or the vultures.

The modern initiation ritual takes place in the church. The person who wants to be initiated formally tells the officials of the Bow Leaders. After hearing the speech the officials accept the person and answer in a formal speech. During this time the date for the initiation ritual is set so that both parties are satisfied with the date. Then it is up to the joining person to look for a god-father and a god-mother to her. The god-parents are usually members in the Bow Leaders, but not always. They can be Bow Leaders from a different village.

The initiation ceremony is carried out in the church around mid-morning. Starting at the church altar the god-parents are on either side of their god-child, the man on the right and the woman on the left. They walk out together to the elder cross in the plaza. They walk from the altar to the elder cross three times going in a counterclockwise direction. The new member is dressed completely in the Bow Leader regalia, including his bow and a quiver with several arrows. After the third trip they stop in front of the church altar and the new member kneels down.

The initiation involves being blessed with a Yaqui rosary and then with a small crucifix. Finally the new member will be pushed down to the floor three times. This concludes the church part of the ritual. Back at the Bow Leaders Headquarters a formal reception speech is given and a feast takes place. There is dancing at intervals. Both the Bow Leaders members and those spectators who are formally requested can dance. However, the first three songs are danced by the captain of the Bow Leaders and two soldiers. After that visitors will be invited to dance. This celebration will continue into the early evening.

Our Bow Leaders group in Yoem Pueblo is still only a few years old and none of the members here in Arizona have gone through a formal initiation. I do not know if they will.

The presence of the Bow Leaders Society in Arizona has always been tenuous. Members of the group probably first came to live in Arizona with other Yaqui refugees who were forced out of their homeland in southern Sonora in the 1890s and early 1900s. During those years around the turn of the century Yaquis suffered brutal oppression from a Mexican government bent on deportation and outright genocide as ways of possessing the rich well-watered farmland of the Yaquis. Thousands of Yaquis were captured and sent to work as slaves in Yucatán. Other Yaquis managed to escape north over the border into southern Arizona. These Yaquis brought many of their cultural traditions with them to this place that some older Yaquis still call "Ringo Bwia," Gringo Land.

During the 1920s a Bow Leaders group formed at the village we now call Old Pascua in Tucson, and they continued to perform through the 1930s. The last remembered performance was in 1941. Edward H. Spicer suggests that because the Bow Leader Society was so tied to *Hiakim*, the Yaqui homeland, it "had no immediate

significance for Yaquis who had decided to forsake the tribal terri-
tory and make their home indefinitely in new and different land."

It may be significant then that recent revival of the Coyote soci-
ety in southern Arizona follows the acquisition of community lands
here. In the 1960s a group of Yaquis acquired title to some 202 acres
from the federal government and moved there to establish the com-
munity known as New Pascua. That community has now grown to
about a thousand acres of land. In 1980 Yaquis living in Yoem
Pueblo were able to purchase the land upon which their village
rests from the private water company that owned it. These small
parts of *Ringo Bwia* are not now and, likely, will never be regarded
as *Hiakim* by Yaquis. But over the more than eighty years they have
lived in southern Arizona Yaquis have named and imagined the
landscape around their communities in ways that echo their home-
land. The revival of the Coyote society may be a sign that they
are ready to take a role as stewards of the space they have been
imagining.

> The first time I heard about the Coyotes was when I was growing up
> in my grandparents' house. My grandparents didn't talk too much
> about them but I remember that they said that they should be called
> the Bow Leaders.
>
> What first interested me about the Bow Leaders was the time in
> 1971, when they were supposed to appear at New Pascua. People were
> excited to hear that a Bow Leaders group was coming from the Yaqui
> country in Sonora to participate in the Christo Rey *pahko*. The night
> of the *pahko*, at that particular time when the Bow Leaders were sup-
> posed to dance, the plaza at New Pascua was packed.
>
> But what was disappointing was that the Bow Leaders did not
> dance. They just sat there. Finally about 1:00 or 2:00 A.M. they began
> to dance. A big circle formed around the area where the group danced.
> What fascinated me was the headdress. I enjoyed watching the way the

hawk feathers flew as the Coyotes danced. The dancers were not very enthusiastic and the singing was hard to hear. So I was not impressed by this group. But what happened in the early morning hours as we drove to our home near Marana did impress me. A coyote ran across the road in front of us. Everybody yelled, "Look, *Wo'i!*"

Yaquis think of the natural world of the Sonoran Desert as one living community. This community is called huya ania, the wilderness world. One of the things that binds those who live in the *huya ania* together is a common language, the language of song. Like deer songs, coyote songs are a part of this language of the wilderness world. They may describe or give a voice to any of the inhabitants of the *huya ania:* coyote, rattlesnake, skunk, badger, fox, dragonfly, crow, vultures, the desert tortoise, to name a few. Others that may be referred to in the songs are *sewa yoleme* (flower person), *yo yoleme* (enchanted person), and *machiwa yoleme* (dawn person). *Yoeme* is the Yaqui word for person. *Yoemem,* People, is what Yaquis call them selves in their own language. The yoemem who appear in the songs—the flower person, the enchanted person, the dawn person— are persons who have special relationships with the other inhabitants of the wilderness world. Coyote songs may also describe the dancers and the objects with which they dance: their headdresses, their bows and arrows. There are songs, too, that are mostly about Christian figures such as Saint Francis, Saint Peter, Saint Paul, Saint John and so on. Felipe considers these songs about the saints to be newer songs.

Like deer songs, the songs of the Bow Leaders have two parts: *u vat weeme,* the first part, which is repeated three or four times or more, and *u tonua,* the concluding part, which is sung once to complete the song. We give only one repetition of the first part for the songs that we transcribe and translate here.

The dancers' movements are keyed to these two parts of the song: the first part is sung over and over as the dancers dance away from the singer, the concluding part as they dance back to the place in front of him where they began. The singer uses a different drum rhythm for each of the two parts. Because of this, it is said that during the concluding part "the drum calls them back," *u kuvahe ameu chai.*

The singer may choose to sing any of the coyote songs that he knows. In that sense, there is no fixed sequence of songs. However, a song called *Sontao Ya'uchim,* Soldier Leaders, is usually the first song sung, and, like deer songs, the other songs follow a progression through evening songs, midnight songs, and morning songs. The subjects of the songs and the manner in which they are danced gets increasingly playful as the night progresses. The songs that we translate here are given in the order in which Felipe sang them at Old Pascua.

The singer accompanies himself with a drum. There is a sounding hole in the rim of the drum, and traditionally the singer sings directly into that hole. It can be difficult, then, to hear exactly what he is saying. This is a performance tradition that singers take advantage of or not depending on the occasion.

BIBLIOGRAPHICAL NOTE

Yaqui Deer Songs Maso Bwikam: A Native American Poetry (Tucson: Sun Tracks and the University of Arizona Press, 1987) tells how we understand our collaboration and the work of translating Yaqui verbal arts for non-Yaqui audiences. In that book, we review earlier attempts to record and translate Yaqui verbal arts, as well as approaches to the translation, interpretation, and appreciation of the verbal arts throughout native America.

Edward H. Spicer's *The Yaquis: A Cultural History* (Tucson: University of Arizona Press, 1980) provides a comprehensive discussion of Yaqui history and culture. See especially pages 164–176 for his discussion of the Coyote Society as protectors of Yaqui lands. Muriel Thayer Painter, *With Good Heart: Yaqui Beliefs and Ceremonies in Pascua Village* (Tucson: University of Arizona Press, 1986), is an encyclopedic work made from the direct testimony of dozens of anonymous Yaqui consultants. We have quoted Refugio Savala, AKA informant "55," from this work. See Felipe S. Molina and Larry Evers, "Muriel Thayer Painter's With Good Heart: Two Views," *Journal of the Southwest*, 29, NO. 1 (Spring 1987), pp. 96 – 106.

Ruth Warner Giddings gathered the only substantive collection of Yaqui narratives as an M.A. thesis under Professor Edward Spicer's direction in 1945. We quote from that work, "Folk Literature of the Yaqui Indians," rather than the version of it that was published as *Yaqui Myths and Legends* (Tucson: University of Arizona Press, 1959). Leticia Varela, an ethnomusicologist at the University of Hermosillo, includes commentary on the Coyote Society in her study *La Musica en La Vida de Los Yaquis* (Hermosillo, Sonora: Secretaria de Fornento Educativo y Cultura, 1986). Of particular interest is her transcription of a formal speech made for initiates to the Bow Leader Society. See pps. 50 – 55.

Amos Taub prepared "Traditional Poetry of the Yaqui Indians," an M.A. thesis (University of Arizona, 1950), under the direction of Edward Spicer and Frances Gillmor.

Sontao Ya'uchim

eme sontao ya'uchim
vanseka
tu'ulisi
chomoka
hisaka

yewi yewima
katema
yewi yewima
katema

katema
katema
katema
katema

vanseka
tu'ulisi
tavelo masata
sialapti
chomoka
hisaka

Soldier Leaders

You soldier leaders
   go ahead
      beautifully
         with the mask
            with the headdress

Out out
   then walk
      out out
         then walk

Walk
   walk
      walk
         walk

Go ahead
   beautifully
      with a parrot wing
         covered green
            with the mask
               with the headdress

yewi yewima
katema
yewi yewima
katema

katema
katema
katema
katema
katema

This song describes the dancers the first time they come out at a ceremony.

Out out
    then walk
        out out
           then walk

Walk
  walk
    walk
      walk
        walk

The first time the bow dancers come out they bless the ground in the four directions: first to the east, then the north, the south, and finally the west. This is called *kusaroapo bwiata teochiuwame,* blessing the earth in the way of the cross. The bow dancers do this because they have a special obligation to protect *Hiakim,* the sacred lands of the Yaquis.

Yoyo Vaka Hiuwa

yoyo vaka hiuwa
yoyo vaka hiuwa

hakunsa vo'oka
masa moye
masa moye

yoyo vaka hiuwa
yoyo vaka hiuwa

hakunsa vo'oka
masa moye
masa moye

masa moye
moye
moye
moye
moye

ayamansu seyewailo saniloapo huyapo
hikatsu vo'oka
masa moye
masa moye

Enchanted Bamboo Arrow

Enchanted enchanted bamboo arrow
  enchanted enchanted bamboo arrow

Where are you lying?
  with wing decaying
    with wing decaying

Enchanted enchanted bamboo arrow
  enchanted enchanted bamboo arrow

Where are you lying?
  with wing decaying
    with wing decaying

Wing decaying
  decaying
    decaying
      decaying
        decaying

Over there in the flower-covered mesquite grove
  on a tree top you are lying
    with wing decaying
      with wing decaying

yoyo vaka hiuwa
yoyo vaka hiuwa

hakunsa vo'oka
masa moye
masa moye

masa moye
moye
moye
moye
moye

Masa, wing, refers to the feathers used as fletching; *vaka*, bamboo, to a local bamboo called *carrizo* in Spanish. *Carrizo* is used for many functions in Yaqui country: the walls of traditional houses are carrizo, canes are split and woven to create baskets and floor mats, flutes are crafted from carrizo, and, as this song suggests, so are arrows.

Enchanted enchanted bamboo arrow
enchanted enchanted bamboo arrow

Where are you lying?
with wing decaying
with wing decaying

Wing decaying
decaying
decaying
decaying
decaying

Refugio Savala recalled a story about a Yaqui woman, Ana Maria, who took a giant Yaqui bowman out to *Tukuluim*, the mountain with the forked peaks that rises above San Carlos Bay, north of Guaymas, Sonora. From *Takalaim* the bowman shot his bow four times to define the boundary of the Yaqui lands. There is a story about another Yaqui bowman who had a contest with the King of Spain during the time of the Conquest. Both shot arrows in the four directions from the center of Yaqui lands. Because the Yaqui shot his arrows farther, the King of Spain gave Yaquis a written title to their land.

Yoyo Vaikumarewi

yoyo vaikumarewi
　　yo va'ata vepasu
　　　　cha'aka
　　　　　　masata yowa

yoyo vaikumarewi
　　yo va'ata vepasu
　　　　cha'aka
　　　　　　haivusu masata yowa

　　masata yowa
　　　　yowa
　　　　　　yowa
　　　　　　　　yowa

　　ayamansu seyewailo
　　　　yo va'ata
　　　　　　maneka vepa
　　　　　　　cha'aka
　　　　　　　　haivusu masata yowa

Enchanted Enchanted Dragonfly

Enchanted enchanted dragonfly
   above the enchanted water
      is hovering
         wing shaking

Enchanted enchanted dragonfly
   above the enchanted water
      is hovering
         wing already shaking

Wing shaking
   shaking
      shaking
         shaking

Over there above the flower-covered
   enchanted water
      where it sits
         it is hovering
            wing already shaking

yoyo vaikumarewi
yo va'ata vepasu
cha'aka
haivusu masata yowa

masata yowa
yowa
yowa
yowa
yowa

Enchanted enchanted dragonfly
    above the enchanted water
        is hovering
            wing already shaking

Wing shaking
      shaking
        shaking
          shaking
            shaking

Kooni Mahai

kooni
    hitasa mahaika
        saiyula vo'oka
           saiyula vo'oka

kooni kooni
    hitasa mahaika
        saiyula vo'oka
           saiyula vo'oka

vo'oka
    vo'oka
        vo'oka
           vo'oka

katikun
    vaka hiuwata mahaika
    wamsu
        saiyula vo'oka

Crow is Afraid

Crow
　what are you afraid of?
　　huddled lying
　　　huddled lying

Crow crow
　what are you afraid of?
　　huddled lying
　　　huddled lying

Lying
　lying
　　lying
　　　lying

Don't you remember
　you are afraid of
　　the bamboo arrow over there?
　　　huddled lying

saiyula vo'oka

kooni kooni
    hitasa mahaika
       saiyula vo'oka
          saiyula vo'oka

vo'oka
   vo'oka
      vo'oka
         vo'oka

Huddled lying

Crow crow
    what are you afraid of?
        huddled lying
           huddled lying

Lying
    lying
        lying
           lying

San Juan San Pasihkota Wiko'i Kottak

San Juan
San Pasihkota wiko'i
su kottak

San Juan
San Pasihkota wiko'i
su kottak

kottak
kottak
kottak
kottak

machiauvicha
su kitteka
haitowikti a
wikeka
kottak

Saint John Broke the Bow of St. Francis

Saint John
    the bow of Saint Francis
        did break

Saint John
    the bow of Saint Francis
        did break

Break
    break
        break
            break

Toward the dawn
    he did stand
        snapped
            pulled
                broke it

machiauvidia
su kitteka
haitowikti a
wikeka
kottak

kottak
kottak
kottak
kottak

In the early 1940s, Lucas Chavez, a singer from Old Pascua, told folklorist Ruth Warner Giddings: *Coyote dancers . . . attend the annual celebrations to San Francis at Magdelena, Sonora . . . they worship the Saint by dancing to a song which praises Saint Francis as a great Yaqui soldier who was able to kill a very powerful bird called* kupahe. *The feathers of this bird are worn in the coyote dancers' headdress.*

Toward the dawn
he did stand
snapped
pulled
broke it

Break
break
break
break

About the same time Refugio Savala told Muriel Thayer Painter: *Another old song refers to San Francisco Xavier being in the army as a soldier. San Pedro is supposed to have borrowed a bow and arrow from San Francisco Xavier and to have pulled on the bow until it broke.*

San Peo Tu'uwata Noka

San Peo
teeka pwetapo kateka
tu'uwata noka

San Peo
teeka pwetapo kateka
tu'uwata noka

noka
noka
noka
noka

ayamansu
seyewailo santo
teweka looria pwetapo katek
tu'uwata noka

San Peo
teeka pwetapo kateka
tu'uwata noka

noka
noka
noka
noka

Refugio Savala, again to Muriel Thayer Painter in the 1940s: [Saint Peter] is supposed to be the captain of the army, and the advisor of the army. He is in a coyote song for dancing, and, in a way, it says that San Pedro sits at the gate of headquarters and advises the soldiers.

Saint Peter Talks About Goodness

Saint Peter
    sitting at heaven's door
        goodness talks

Saint Peter
    sitting at heaven's door
        goodness talks

Talks
    talks
        talks
            talks

Over there
    sitting at the flower-covered
        holy heaven's door
            goodness talks

Saint Peter
    sitting at heaven's door
        goodness talks

Talks
    talks
        talks
            talks

Hepela

eme sontao ya'uchim
tulisi hepela
kateka
nausu yewe
nausu yewe

eme sontao ya'uchim
tulisi hepela
kateka
nausu yewe
nausu yewe

yewe
yewe
yewe
yewe

imsu sewa votsu
hepela kateka
nausu yewe

Side by Side

You soldier leaders
    beautifully side by side
        are walking
            together playing
                together playing

You soldier leaders
    beautifully side by side
        are walking
            together playing
                together playing

Playing
    playing
        playing
            playing

Here on the flower road
    side by side you are walking
        together playing

eme sontao ya'uchim
tulisi hepela
kateka
nausu yewe
nausu yewe

yewe
yewe
yewe
yewe

The Bow Leaders dance three at a time. Their usual formation is not *natchaka kade*, one after the other walking, or *mochala*, bunched up as in a crowd, but rather, as this song describes them, *hepela*, side by side.

You soldier leaders
   beautifully side by side
      are walking
         together playing
            together playing

Playing
   playing
      playing
         playing

Side by side, in rhythm and perfectly in step is the definitive posture of their dance. But like the deer dancer and the *pahkolam* they may perform *yeuwame,* plays, in which they act out certain songs. In one, often performed near the end of the *pahko,* the people who are giving the *pahko* put out a plate of barbecued meat on the ground between the singer and the dancers. The singer sings about coyotes as the dancers dance out in their usual way, then turn around and dance in backward, dropping to all fours only at the last instant and fighting like coyotes over the plate of meat. Then they resume dancing in their usual position, *hepela,* side by side, but now one coyote has meat in his mouth.

Yoyo A'akame

yoyo a'akame
  sevipo vo'oka

siirisiiriti hia
  siirisiiriti hia
    siirisiiriti hia

hia
  hia
    hia
      hia

katikun
  taewalita sumeiyaka
    haivusu sevipo vo'oka

siirisiiriti hia
  siirisiiriti hia
    siirisiiriti hia

hia
  hia
    hia
      hia

The word for rattles is *ayam*.

Enchanted Enchanted Rattlesnake

Enchanted enchanted rattlesnake
in the cactus is lying

Siirisiiri sounding
siirisiiri sounding
siirisiiri sounding

Sounding
sounding
sounding
sounding

Remember
he is frightened of the day
already in the cactus lying

Siirisiiri sounding
siirisiiri sounding
siirisiiri sounding

Sounding
sounding
sounding
sounding

This is a play song. When Felipe sings it, the dancers dance all the way out during the repetitions of the first stanza as usual but when the concluding stanza begins, "when the drum calls them back," they get down on the ground and slither like snakes.

Hupa

hupa
    hu'upa kutapo
      kateka

to'e to'eti hia
    to'e to'eti hia
      to'e to'eti hia

hia
    hia
      hia
        hia

katikun
    yo hu'upapo
      kateka

hupa
    hu'upa kutapo
      kateka

Skunk

Skunk
on the mesquite wood
is sitting

To'e to'e sounding
to'e to'e sounding
to'e to'e sounding

Sounding
sounding
sounding
sounding

Remember
on the enchanted mesquite
he is sitting sounding

Skunk
on the mesquite wood
is sitting

to'e to'eti hia
to'e to'eti hia
to'e to'eti hia

hia
hia
hia
hia

Some older Yaquis use a tongue twister that plays with sounds like this song. The tongue twister goes like this:

hupa hu'upapo	skunk in mesquite
vetuku kateka	under sitting
huvam huhak	stinky farted

To'e to'e sounding
    to'e to'e sounding
      to'e to'e sounding

Sounding
    sounding
      sounding
       sounding

Sherman Alexie

The Native American Broadcasting System

1

Five hundred years from now, archaeologists will discover
a bowling ball buried beside the body of an Indian chief.

Research papers will be published in the academic journals prov-
ing the existence of a large fifteen-pound globe-like organ
in a majority of late twentieth century Native Americans.

"Although the organ itself was petrified," states an expert,
"We were able to ascertain that its purpose was to absorb excess
quantities of fluids, most likely alcoholic in nature."

2

NEWS BULLETIN: The American Academy of Motion Picture Arts
and Sciences has announced the establishment of a new
category for this year's Academy Awards: Best Performance
by a Non-Native in a Native American Role. Nominees this year
include Burt Lancaster, Charles Bronson, Trevor Howard, Burt
Reynolds, and Kevin Costner.

VISIT TEEPEE TOWN

3

The reservation penny still lying on the ground
   with no Indian left around
to bend down and pick it up and it's a buffalo
   penny (what a coincidence)
so when you flip it, chances are even
   you'll still see Lincoln.
So what's left but to leave the damn thing
   where it belongs, under
our feet, collecting dust, sticking to the bare feet
   of Indian children who don't
have any shoes, socks, or even the smallest wet dream?

4

Baby, come make me promises, come
close and whisper to me of land claims
uranium mines and tax-free cigarettes.
Baby, hold my hand when we cross the Spokane River
into the United States of America, kiss me
in the dark, fuck me against the back wall of a 7-11.

5

Custer came back to life in Spokane managing the Copper Penny
Grocery, stocked the rubbing alcohol next to the cheap wine:

RUBBING ALCOHOL 99¢

THUNDERBIRD WINE $1.24

The urban Indians shuffle in with tattered coats and boots,
counting quarters while Custer trades food stamps for cash,
offering absolution.

6

The old man on the Greyhound asks me why
so many Indians ride the bus. I tell him
it's about loneliness, all about loneliness.

The old man on the Greyhound asks me if
I know what that word means. I tell him
it's the sound of glass breaking, dust
from smallpox blankets filling the lungs
horses exploding beneath wheels, houses
swallowing up all the cold air, children
running bareback through barbed wire, hearts
pounding under glass in the pawn shop.

The old man on the Greyhound asks me where
I've been, where I'm going. I tell him
I just got back from pissing in the Atlantic
and I'm traveling to the exact edge
of the West to piss in the Pacific.
Everybody has to have a mission.

VISIT TEEPEE TOWN

7

NEWS BULLETIN: Thirteen heavily armed Native Americans
stormed the beach at Liberty Island today and inverted
the Statue of Liberty.

8

And where do we go from here? All I know
        is that I hide myself in
Lester FallsApart's right shoe, waiting
        for the next General Assistance
check, cussing at all the Indians passed out
        half-assed awake, listening
and believing that Lester's goddamn right shoe
        can talk, can make campaign
promises, invent slogans, report baseball scores
        the weather, the father who
killed his family with a spoon, knife, and two forks.

9

I am the essence of powwow, I am
toilets without paper, I am fry bread
in sawdust, I am bull dung
on rodeo grounds at the All-Indian
Rodeo and Horse Show, I am

the essence of powwow, I am
video games with braids, I am spit
from toothless mouths, I am turquoise
and bootleg whiskey, both selling
for twenty bucks a swallow, I am

the essence of powwow, I am
fancydancers in flannel, I am host drum
amplified, I am *Fuck you*
don't come back and *Leave me*

the last hard drink. I am
the essence of powwow, I am the dream
you lace your shoes with, I am
the lust between your toes, I am
the memory you feel across the bottom
of your feet whenever you walk too close.

10

NEWS BULLETIN: The Adolph Coors Corporation is sponsoring a
new promotional contest. On the bottom inside of every beer can
and bottle, Coors has printed a single letter. The first Indian to
collect and spell out the word RESERVATION will receive a train
ticket for a special traveling back 555 years.

11

Buffalo Bill came back to life and hunted pianos.
During a period of roughly 25 years, he shot 3 million
pianos west of the Mississippi alone. An old-timer
remembers the summer he was trapped on a boulder

on the plains when the Great Northern Piano Herd
passed by him. There were pianos as far as the eye
could see, pianos upon pianos, all wild and within
an arm's length, pianos from horizon to horizon.

12

There could be a global nuclear war
       and the last white man
left alive would convince himself he was Cherokee
       and would travel from
monument to monument, reinventing his own personal
       Trail of Tears, invite his feet
to stomp a new and improved dust down into
       the ground, print up a T-shirt
advertising it all for nobody: the First Annual
       All-Indian, Six-Foot-and-Under
45-Years-and-Over Trail of Tears Revisited.

13

Baby, don't leave me in the in-between, between
window panes, I-90 and Highway 2, red and white
cash and credit, here and there, this and that
treaty and Sand Creek, between Thunderbird wine
and rubbing alcohol, artificial turf and grass
the dreams you save and the dreams you pawn.
Baby, don't leave me in the in-between, between
the bilateral symmetries of love and lust.

14

Don't judge a man until you've walked a mile
       in his moccasins, you call it corn
we call it maize, don't litter or Iron Eyes Cody
       will shed a solitary tear

do as the great Indian chiefs of the past
    and leave everything
the way you found it but nobody loves a drunken Indian
    anger in his heart, bitter
and more than a little confused, give him a uniform
    a medal from Iwo Jima, a flag
folded into a box, give him a pair of combat boots
    so damn big he can use them
as a foxhole, give him a pair of Army socks so dry
    and tight and white they never
get themselves dirty, give him a book on survival
    and cut out the last chapter
give him a pair of glasses that reflect back so he can
    only see his eyes lying
again, give him a parade through the reservation
    so the Indian children will finally
receive their visions, give him a blind horse
    who isn't afraid of trees
give him a car without brakes or a steering wheel
    give him a ticket to the symphony
and tell him all the flutes are snakes, give him
    a basketball and tell him
to play his way off the reservation, give him a manual
    for home improvement
without a table of contents, steal all his hammers
    and nails, give him keys
to a door, a door that don't belong to no house.

VISIT TEEPEE TOWN

15
Baby, come make me promises, tell me
you'll love me as long as
the winds blow
the grasses grow
the rivers flow.

Juan Felipe Herrera

Nothing Is Taken That Is Not Given

ODE TO THE TRAVELING MEN

The rap beat of Arrested Development flared through the red-dish walls of Kayum Mario's house. We drank and saluted each other. More Mexican Winstons, one after another, out of their shiny red package. I didn't think of the boys' ages or whether they smoked. The thought that the Lacandón harvest tobacco and use it for cere-monial occasions, where it cuts across status and generations, or that even smoking a cigarette could have many meanings, did not cross my mind. I had no rationale. I offered them a smoke out of a crazy exhilaration and separateness that I felt. I had arrived at Kayum's house; would I be welcomed?

Kayum Mario's lightness made me think of my son Joaquín, the boy I had known briefly in Venice, California, before his mother and I separated in 1970, a year after our marriage. She was a woman from Queens whom I met during my first year of college at UCLA. I didn't see Joaquín again for nineteen years, until I received a letter from his mother in 1989 asking forgiveness for banishing me from him and inviting me to visit them in upstate New York. I hadn't mentioned all this to myself for a while. This was buried too, along with my mother and father.

Following my divorce in the early seventies, I had remarried twice in California. The second marriage was a turbulent affair with a woman with whom I had had a daughter, Alma. In time we divorced as well, and still—not knowing how to communicate or what it was I wanted in a partner—I married a woman from the Pacific Northwest. This liaison ended with my predictable three-year quandaries and foibles. Finally, in 1983, I met Margarita Luna Robles and fought out and cried out my pain. I learned to let myself love and be loved. By the late eighties, I met Joaquín again, now twenty-one years old, and my second son, Joshua, also from my first marriage, whom I had never seen.

I thought of my distant sons and daughter as I listened to Kayum Mario's laughter. I thought of my stepchildren, Marlene and Robert. I could see all my children at ease in Nahá, running down La Ruta or carving a face out of a chunk of caoba. I could see them in their true form. Another romantic illusion punished me.

Just got off the Tumbo from Ocosingo.

I was retracing Trudi Blom's trail that she laid down with Frans in the forties, I was going over the conquest routes to El Próspero. I wanted to excavate into their motives and fascinations; their own dreaming and jottings. I was asking for their lost pages of the shriveled colonias propped up on stilts and swollen vines. I came off the bus, waving good-bye to the machete man, the one I broke a bolillo with. I fell out and ran to the edge of La Ruta with my bags and the ancient hammock Doña América let me borrow back at Na Bolom. I found three young boys full of smiles and lost resemblances. I found my mother drifting by me and the children that I had yanked out of my bones many years ago. Pain and desire in the mix of an unfettered smooth selva heat.

"My father will be here pretty soon," Kayum Mario said. "Don't worry." Kayum Mario took a deep drag, turned his head up to the sky, blew the smoke out. The rap soundtrack to *Malcolm X* bounced through the giant satellite ear and played itself in the hot vegetation curled around us. Another drink of cañabrava. Kayum Mario told me he had been to Los Angeles with his father. "They invite us every now and then," he said. "My father just won the Chiapas Prize. They gave him eight million pesos."

Chan K'in José and Chan K'in Francisco fiddled with their cigarettes as Kayum Mario provided me with an informal resume. I noticed his Spanish. He rolled his Ws and used the Castillian zeta. I wanted to ask him about his facility with the language. In 1970 only a few of the elders spoke in Spanish. I stopped myself. Stopped

asking
the native questions
    about his progress. I caught myself acting out an old colonial
    gesture,
following the hardened tradition of anthropologists and "native"
    seekers: traveling men with swords, bibles, machetes, and notes,
traveling men with satchels and journals and blurred maps, ham-
mers, and mosquito nets between themselves and their project, their
sturdy objects of study; their language thefts for the sake of an
enlightened Europe and "High" America.

    Grand Excavators,
    High Voiced Speakers-for-the-Object,
    Commanders of the New Colony,
    Tomb-Gatherers,
    Shard Experts,
    Ink Drinkers of the New World,
    Civilizer-Surgeons,
    Indian Carnival Cartographers,

Journalists of the Sacred Drinking Gourd,
Filmmakers for the Archaeology of Usurpation,
Oil Vampire Drillers with a Holy Book of Salvation
and a mask of Ecological Harmony.

No more questions.
No more cameras.
No more film

No more recordings or picking up the latest net bag from the shelf.
I sickened myself with my own grand quests. I caught myself in my
own seeker thirst and seeker suction. Chan K'in José's words about
my mother resounded through me.

    Visit, he had said.

    She *visits* you often

    She *visits* you.

    I realized the beauty of my dreams, the follies of my self-made
utopias. There was no need for my bag of equipment.

    After twenty-three years of going over my memory notes on
Nahá, I dropped my nylon bag of intentions. I dropped the archaic
grammar of conquest. There was nothing to translate, nothing to
take back. How could I take back what Chan K'in José has given
me? How could I take back the cropped greenness of the caoba
trees or the stillness of the lakes, the deepness of the oil drills?

    Here were the initial questions:

    Who will read?

    Is reading enough?

    Take back and leave what?

    Take what from whom?

    Take back to what?

What did the Mayan Takers cull from la selva?
Whom did they represent in the last five centuries?
How do we listen?
What satellite dish has received the news?

I thought of the Traveling Men who had passed through these
Mayan regions:

Don Diego de Vera Ordoñez de Villaquirán, visionary of El Próspero
Fray Diego de Landa of the Franciscan Order
John Lloyd Stephens, the American traveler
Frederick Catherwood, Stephens's English artist companion
Alfred Maudsley, the English explorer
Sylvanus Griswold Morley, the American archaeologist
Alfred Tozzer, the Harvard archaeologist
Charles Olson, the American Black Mountain poet
John Teeple, the American astronomer
Frans Blom, the Swiss mapmaker and selva stepper
Allen Ginsberg, the Beat Sutra singer
Hermann Beyer, the American Mayan hieroglyphic reader
Sir Eric Thompson, the British New World archaeologist
Heinrich Berlin, the German epigraphist, expert of Palenque
Yurii Knorosov, the Soviet linguist
William Coe, the American archaeologist
Ian Graham, Coe's American colleague
Roberto D. Bruce, the American Lacandón anthropologist
Victor Perera, the Jewish American journalist
Juan Felipe Herrera, the Chicano poet with a funny face

How can we unearth the Mayan language from four thousand years
of drift outside the epicenter, in the highlands of Guatemala, from

its split into thirty-one distinct tongues, from its channels into Yucatecan and Cholan, subgroups that spread northeast of the highlands into what is now sectored as the tiny northern village of Nahá and its southern neighbor, Lacanjá Chan Sayab?

How did these Traveling Men leave these sites, these tombs, these burial mounds, these loud stone mouth slabs and stele, how did they leave the broken villages of chapay, guatapil, and sival?

What was the cost?

What New World language did these Traveling Men edify, reconstruct, and translate?

What Travelers New World Brittanica did they contribute to? In what museums and culture boxes is it housed?

What is the shape of this revered monument given to us by these New World Traveling Men?

To what unleashed codex do the ones left behind run to?

Could the Lacandones, the ones we quickly see as the "silent subjects" of Mesoamerican research, also be the "speaking subjects?" Speakers for themselves—across cultural boundaries in time and space? And the 999,500 non-Lacandón Maya of Chiapas?

Nothing can be taken, only given.

Nothing was taken that was not given.

Greg Sarris

The Verbal Art of Mabel McKay:
Talk as Culture Contact and Cultural Critique

For years Mabel McKay has been pursued by countless people who want to know about her world. As the only surviving member of the Long Valley Cache Creek Pomo tribe and the last of the Bole Maru Dreamers, she is seen as a repository of valuable information: anthropologists seek ethnographic data; linguists want to record her language; and still others want to know about shamanism and the dream world. Yet her responses to questions are maddening.

"What do you do for poison oak?" a student once asked in a large auditorium where Mabel was being interviewed as a native healer. "Calamine lotion," Mabel answered.

In another instance Mabel was asked to speak before a group of Stanford medical students who wanted to know about "ethnic medicine" and how they might work cooperatively with native healers. She smoked a cigarette on stage while waiting to be introduced. Once she was introduced she rubbed out her cigarette in the tin ashtray a student found for her, set the ashtray on the floor, stood up and said, "I have to pray first." She prayed and sang a song, all of which lasted about five minutes, then sat down and talked somewhat in a trance about the dictates of her spirit and her doctoring. Then suddenly she stopped and looked up, out to the audience. "Okay," she said, "now who can tell me what I just said?" Her audience was quiet, stunned. "Ain't nobody got a word for me?" she asked finally and laughed. "I thought you wanted to know about healers." One student spoke up and paraphrased a portion of Mabel's presentation, reinforcing Mabel's legitimate claim to be a teacher rather than a naive informant. Then another student challenged the dynamic Mabel had established by asking how she became a doctor. "Like you," she said, "long time studying!"

In the first instance Mabel answered the question (about poison oak) but, at the same time, renegotiated the representation of reality that the question presented. In answering the student's question, she acknowledged that she is Indian but, at the same time, introduced the fact she is a contemporary American, which redefined the student's notion of "Indian." In the latter instance she challenged the assumption that the students could take information without having to account for it. The students were prepared to take notes and get answers, but could they say what those answers meant, as Mabel understood them and wanted them understood? Here she interrupted the classic participant-observation method.

While Mabel may not give so-called straight answers, she continues to answer. Until a recent bout with arthritis, she traveled regularly, demonstrating basketry and talking about her art and culture. She enjoyed interviews and told stories about the "ancient times" and about her life and people and places she has known. Always she insisted that it "is important for people to know." If her interlocutors find themselves baffled by her talk, it must have something to do with knowing or, more precisely, how people are to know. Again, by talk I include all speech categories—responses to questions, gossip, idle chitchat, stories—that Mabel may use in conversation with others, since, as I hope to demonstrate, the various categories engender the same effect. The talk establishes the premises on which an understanding of her world can begin, and an examination of this talk reveals, I think, just how those premises are established and in what ways they are significant.

Talk as such raises the question of talk as performance, specifically in terms of Richard Bauman's notion of performance as a distinct communicative phenomenon whereby "performance sets up, or represents, an interpretive frame within which the messages being communicated are to be understood [so that] this frame contrasts with at least one other frame, the literal." The frame is in this sense metacommunicative; the speaker's use of a special code, perhaps the attribution of an archaism or special formula (e.g., "once upon a time"), keys the nature of the event or performance (genre) and how the interlocutor is to respond. Hence the interlocutor knows "this is a story" or "this is a joke" and subsequently has expectations associated with the respective keyed speech event. For the ethnographer or folklorist Bauman suggests "the essential task in the ethnography of performance is to determine the culture-specific constellations of communicative means that serve to key performance in particular communities." Ideally, fieldworkers would acquire keys to the "entire domain, viewing speaking and performing as a cultural system and indicating how the whole range of performance is keyed." Yet Bauman is quick to point out that such perfect, standardized ethnographies—where certain keys always indicate certain speech events—cannot account for the individuality of each speech event or, more important, for my discussion here, for how the speaker may manipulate certain frames given the context in which she is speaking, particularly if that context is new or unusual in some way. I am thinking of what Dell Hymes (1981) calls *metaphrasis*, where a speaker can use the "structural, conventional performance system itself as a resource for creative manipulation, as a base on which a range of communicative transformations can be wrought." The structure of performance events can change, or new structures may emerge, depending on particular contextual conditions. If one considers the presence of a fieldworker as real, and thus a variable, in the so-called native domain, what constitutes a frame in the speech event the fieldworker records and describes is likely to depend and to emerge from that specific context. The fieldworker cannot know about frames independent of his or her presence. What the fieldworker sees is not so much how the entire community keys speech events for its members but rather how it keys them for the fieldworker specifically.

If Mabel is performing in ways that are specific to the Cache Creek Pomo, there is little way of knowing. The fact that she is using English may necessarily preclude the presence of the native form as such. What is known is that her speech activities, at least in what I have related thus far, point to the frames her interlocutors are using to understand her. It is difficult to discern the extent to which Mabel is performing, or if and to what degree her activity is intentional, because she forces her interlocutors to examine presuppositions that shaped and are embedded in their questions.

To illustrate how a fieldworker's presence can generate emergent forms of framing activity on the part of the informant, and to further discuss Mabel's talk, I want to take a cursory glance at Robert Oswalt's *Kashaya Texts*. Perhaps along with S.A. Barrett's *Pomo Myths*, *Kashaya Texts* is the most complete collection of Pomo literature in one text. Of interest is the fact that the book is primarily a study in linguistics and includes the Pomo text with the English translation. Also the text comprises stories from one tribe of Pomo (Kashaya) told largely by just two informants, Herman James and Essie Parrish. Perhaps the most notable feature of all the speech events, regardless of Oswalt's categories (i.e. Myth, The Supernatural, Folk History, Miscellany) or how James and Parrish might themselves categorize a story they are telling (e.g., "This is a story from the old days" or "Now I'm going to tell about something I did"), is James's and Parrish's uses of formal frames to open and close their talk.

In the first text, titled by Oswalt "The Creation of the Ocean," Herman James begins: "This is something from ancient times— I am going to tell about the creation." James concludes the narrative stating, "This is the end of my account of the start of the world in the old days and the making of the ocean—that is what I have been telling about. This is finally the end." In another story titled by Oswalt "The Flood," Essie Parrish begins, "I am now going to tell about people turning into trees at the time of destruction" and concludes with "This is all." Oswalt observes that the narratives told by James and Parrish differ most notably in the endings: "Essie Parrish usually terminates a story rather abruptly with a phrase like 'This is the end.' Herman James employs such phrases but typically precedes them with often-repeated protestations of the truth of the story." In concluding his telling of a long story associated with "The Flood" and titled by Oswalt "The Whale in the Creek," James, for example, declares:

> This is also a true story. It really happened. This is what my grandmother said when she told it. I listened when she told me. "It is true," she said. That is why we believe it and tell it too. This is a true story. This is the end.

It seems that though Essie Parrish, too, often repeats protestations of the truth, albeit more subtly, as in the case of "The Flood," where she says before closing with "This is all" that "Our old people used to tell us about it, saying that's the way it was [and why] that mountain is taboo." Still, in the case of either James or Parrish, the use of formal frames is standard. Sometimes Parrish or James might open by setting the scene, perhaps by giving the location of the action. But even short descriptions of activities, such as "Preparing Buckeye," end abruptly. Parrish begins, "I am going to talk about preparing buckeyes" *(bahsa dutatoc e a dici duwan k'e),* and after a brief description of the process says, "this is all" *(mu ma a e me p i),* just as she does when closing a mythic story. Here myth and description of daily activity—indeed all genres of speech—meet on common ground. We may find terms such as *duwi dici du* (telling about Coyote or Coyote stories), which might be said to serve as special codes keying genre (i.e., Coyote stories), but these terms, often occurring at the beginning of the narrative, do not affect the formal frames opening and closing the texts.

This framing activity had something to do with the context in which the stories were produced. Oswalt's "original purpose in collecting the texts was to provide a corpus for the study of languages." He wanted language, linguistic units that he could study and translate, and that is exactly what he got—stories that are rendered as separate and complete units, framed so that Oswalt has the story but no context beyond the story in which to understand it. He has information, but it is not engaged with the world from which the information comes. I doubt that Mrs. Parrish would use the same abrupt frames when telling family members about preparing buckeyes. In my entire experience with Mrs. Parrish and among the Kashaya Pomo—nearly thirty years—I have never heard such frames used in English or Kashaya, except in very formal situations, where Mrs. Parrish was preaching to a large Kashaya congregation, and then the situation was again quite different. And just recently when

I asked her daughter, Violet Parrish Chappell, about these texts and their frames, she replied, "Mom just did it that way, for the language. He [Oswalt] wanted language. I heard those stories differently— when Mom used to tell them when we kids were in bed."

But one must also consider the possibility that such framing devices emergent in this context, are also convenient for James and Parrish. Information regarding formalized or "traditional" Pomo storytelling is scanty. Both Mabel McKay and Essie Parrish have talked about listening to old-time storytellers where "you had to sit on the floor and listen. Parrish told Oswalt, "they [old-time story-tellers] say that it is dangerous to relate Coyote stories while sitting up." Any attempt on the part of fieldworkers to recreate the "native scene" risks the danger of denying the present, of displacing the significance of the field-workers' presence and how it affects the speakers' and ultimately the fieldworkers' re-creation of the text. In this instance with James and Parrish, we might examine rules and ethics of behavior that are still endemic to the Pomo, particularly as they might affect how a story is told. Mabel, for instance, mentions regularly that she cannot tell Coyote stories during the summer months. "It is forbidden," she says. "It's an old-time rule. Us old people know that." Equally significant is the pervasive notion of privacy among the Pomo, particularly in terms of sacred objects, songs, and stories. A person's songs and stories are considered valu-able property not to be shared openly with strangers. Sacred objects are never handled or touched except by their owners. Given just these strictures we might imagine why James and Parrish presented the stories the way they did to Oswalt, who did virtually all of his fieldwork in the summer months. James and Parrish, as elders and religious people, were in the position of being asked to break taboo and disregard an invasion of privacy. What resulted was a text that reflected at least to some degree, that situation; the texts, as already suggested, are framed so that they are closed ("This is all"), thus inviting neither further storytelling nor inquiry into their world.

While Bauman and others acknowledge the possibility of emergent forms, particularly in new situations, or, as Bauman notes, "under conditions of change," they still tacitly assume, somehow discounting their presence as recorders/interpreters, that a "true structure (Hymes 1981)" can be discerned. Dell Hymes's "major purpose is to argue for the systematic study of variation in performance" whereby he can compare various textualized forms of the same tale to discover the true, or "authoritative," text. Dan Ben-Amos argues for a kind of holism where fieldworkers should examine "the set of contrastive attributes (thematic, behavioral) [that] represent the structure of relations between distinct genres in the system of folklore communication." Yet if Hymes were to study the variations in performance as discerned solely in the textualized narratives of James and Parrish, what would emerge as an authoritative text would not be a text native to the Kashaya Pomo but to the Kashaya Pomo and a fieldworker, in this case James or Parrish and Oswalt. The contrastive elements that Ben-Amos would discover to determine Kashaya genres of speech would be those predicated on the presence of Oswalt. What we are given by James and Parrish is something like a note on the door describing what is inside, although the door itself is closed.

If, in this instance, James and Parrish close discourse about their world, Mabel does something quite different. Where James and Parrish present stories as isolated pieces of information devoid of meaningful contexts in which we might understand them, including the opportunity to question, Mabel McKay, as pointed out, makes the interlocutor immediately aware of the present context and of the ways the interlocutor may be framing her world, which does not close the discourse but exposes the chasms between two interpretive worlds over which the discourse must continue. Whether the interlocutor is a student, friend, ethnographer, or myself, the dynamic of Mabel's talk remains characteristically the same. Granted we are left to read textualized versions of James's and Parrish's texts, and there my analogy may appear shaky in its attempt to illustrate the difference here, but perhaps that is precisely why Mabel will not allow herself to be recorded—she will not be absent from any discussion of her world. Consider again some examples of her talk.

Mabel has just finished talking about dreaming to a group of non-Indian, Marin County people interested in Pomo culture. A middle-aged woman asks if it is the spirit that keeps Mabel young-looking and what tips Mabel or the spirit might have for maintaining a youthful appearance. "You should try dying your hair," Mabel answers. After Mabel has explained how she met Essie Parrish in a dream twenty years before she had met her in person, Mabel was asked if she recognized Mrs. Parrish when Mrs. Parrish walked into the room. "Yes," Mabel answered, "but I think she cut her hair a little." In another instance, where she is talking to a group of social scientists, Mabel tells about a famous Indian doctor who was notorious for escaping from the Lake County jail. Many people claimed he turned into a horsefly and flew through the cell bars. "Do you believe that?" a psychiatrist asked. "No," Mabel says with a laugh before adding earnestly, "I believe he went down the toilet." In a basket-weaving demonstration at Stanford University, Mabel talks about how she must pray for all the materials she gathers (for basket making), and a student asks if she talks to plants. "Yes, if I have to use them," she answers.

"Do plants talk to one another?"

"I suppose."

"What do they say [to one another]?"

Mabel laughs. "How do I know? Why would I be listening?"

Any discussion of frames and keying brings to mind Irving Goffman's Frame Analysis, in which he discusses the ways in which a particular strip of activity can be keyed and rekeyed. I am thinking specifically of what Goffman calls a fabrication, or "the intentional effort of one or more individuals to manage activity so that a party of one or more others will be induced to have a false belief about what it is that is going on. Those taken in can be said to be contained." Goffman continues "that for those in on a deception, what is going on is fabrication; for those contained what is going on is what is being fabricated." What is essential here is that both parties operate in terms of the rules and premises of a primary framework. And that is the point Mabel elucidates—that she and her interlocutors are not operating from the rules and premises of the same primary framework. Again, questions regarding Mabel's intentionality are difficult, and, I would argue, unnecessary, to answer. But she is not tricking or fabricating; her talk points to what constitutes difference. In the above examples of her talk, as with the examples I cited at the start of this essay, Mabel is responding to questions, and her responses expose that which is embedded in the question that accounts for the rifts between her world and that of her interlocutors.

What happens with longer forms of talk, say the stories Mabel tells? Here for purposes of my discussion I am arbitrarily separating longer forms—stories and extended conversations—from other forms—idle chitchat and responses to questions—since in reality they are often integral to one another in a variety of ways. Concerning a tale or anecdote, or what he calls "a replaying," Goffman claims it "will be something that listeners emphatically insert themselves into, vicariously reexperiencing what took place." If the longer speech events are associated with, and engender the same effects as, the shorter ones, as I am suggesting, it is not emphatic identification and vicarious reexperience that Mabel's tales and anecdotes elicit but rather the limits of such.

As mentioned, I have heard her stories since I was a child, since that first day I walked into her home with Marshall, her adopted son, and heard her talking to some woman about a sacred mountain. But it wasn't until one winter evening during a visit home from college that I began thinking seriously about Mabel and the nature of her talk. I think the story of the visit can illustrate how the longer and shorter speech events resemble one another and, at the same time, further my exploration of Mabel McKay's talk.

First a story.

What happened, a man poisoned.

See, them girls' grandmother, _____'s mother, she got fixed that way. How it happened, a man poisoned her.

He wanted her, this man. She was beautiful, but she would do like this: doctor somebody, then get up and leave her equipment. If she liked a man she would do it like that: get up and get out of the way. Maybe not come back until the next day.

Well, this man, he wanted her. But she was already married to another man, _____. She said, "I don't want you." See, he was old at that time already. He was an old man and I guess she liked the younger men, I don't know [chuckling].

He got mad then. He told her, don't be fooling around no more, no leaving your doctoring here and there.

Then I don't know what happened, but she got pregnant AGAIN. Some older man, not her husband, I understand.

Then HE got mad. He got REAL mad. Then he got sick, the old man. Send for _____, he was saying: I'm dying and I need her to pray, he was telling somebody.

So she went there. And that's how it happened, they say. He tricked her, took something of hers while she was singing—I don't know what, maybe a pipe, cocoon, something anyway—and fixed her with it. And that's how they found her in the morning. She was already dead with that baby, frozen they say. And he's the one cursed them all with that manwild business. For generations, he was saying.

Anyone familiar with Pomo lore and ethnography might discern recognizable features in this story. E.W. Aginsky noted that "there is no phase of Pomo life that [he] could discover which did not have some taboos connected with it" and "that every death and misfortune was the result of indirect or direct retaliation from (1) the 'supernaturals' or (2) from some individual." According to Bean and Theodoratus, "illness could be caused by ghosts but was most often caused by poisoning." Depending on the different ethnographical descriptions used and how the story is viewed in terms of those descriptions, the typical and atypical Pomo features can be discussed endlessly. Likewise, a closer reading of the text might suggest ways that elements of language and narrative format determine meaning. Deconstruction would unveil Mabel's hidden agenda.

Mabel told me this story about the man who poisoned the beautiful woman doctor when I was trying to solicit answers from her to questions raised by a professor of mine. He had "done some work on the Pomo"—we read his article in an introductory anthropology course—and he was impressed that I knew Mabel McKay, whom he deemed "impossible to crack." He gave me a list of questions about doctoring and the use of crystals and herbs. Mabel promptly circumvented the questions. It must have appeared odd to her that I was suddenly interested in such things. Then again she knew I had been to the university, and now seeing me at home for the first time, she may not have been so surprised. After all, she had more experience with college than I. She had been answering student and faculty questions for over forty years.

I remember it was quite late. I looked at the clock above her head on the kitchen wall. It was raining too, and though I lived only a couple of miles up the road, I wanted to get on.

"Now what was I saying? Oh, yeah. About the laundry. Do you know _____?"

Thinking of home, I had not been following. For the last hour I had contented myself with this same idle chitchat about people and daily routine. I was tired. "Yes," I said, finally catching up with her. I told her how I knew the woman's daughters in high school. Marshall and I both had known the girls.

"Oh, yes?" Mabel took a sip of her coffee, then set her cup carefully on the table. "Hmmm," she said. "Well, I seen her for the first time today, first time since she was a girl. At the laundromat I seen her. She said to me, 'Are you Mabel?' I said, 'Yes.' Then I seen who it was.

"It happened I seen her coming. I seen her in the car with those grandkids, the black ones. She was trying to hide them from me, even yet. Keeping them in the car when she was talking to me. Looking around to see if they jumped out. It was funny the way she did that.

"After while Marshall says, 'Who is that, Mama?' I say it's relatives, some kind. He says, 'Oh, do we have to claim them too?' I start laughing [chuckling]. 'Yeah,' I said, 'we do.'

"Well, not all relatives that way, but way her mother, _____, took in Grandma dancing up there by that place they call Rattlesnake Island."

I tried to explain why Marshall might feel the way he did. I made a few derogatory remarks about the woman's loose daughters and about the woman's sister, the girls' aunt, who got stuck between the bars in the county jail while reaching for a man in another cell.

Mabel looked up, over her glasses, admonishing. "You don't know the whole story," she said. "What happened, a man poisoned . . ."

Paul Ricoeur suggests "the absolute here and now" of the dialogical "we" is "shattered by writing." By inserting the context of the storytelling event here, which, granted, the reader must accept secondhand, I feel I can at least produce a representation of the dialogical "we." This representation helps to illustrate how the story, like the shorter speech events cited earlier, interrupts preconceived notions on the part of the interlocutor. The story was not a response to a question but rather a response to a statement made about the subject of a conversation. Intentional or not, the story commented upon a specific statement about the subject and simultaneously pointed beyond the statement and immediate subject. If I had to reconsider how I saw the girls in the story, I would also have to reconsider how I saw other things—doctoring, crystals, and herbs. The story opens dialogue about two personal and cultural worlds, exposing what makes for the "we" in "the absolute here and now."

Here I am not simply indicating the limits of a text centered approach nor extolling the virtues of contextual studies. It is the dynamic of the speech event in context that I am talking about, not as it may be geared to a particular person or persons, say, with a specific moral in tow, but as it works to establish a premise from which a moral or ethic emerges. Anyone with whom Mabel is speaking can experience this dynamic. The speech event can interrupt and simultaneously expose the interlocutor's presuppositions at any point—in a single response to a question, in a story, or at some point in a conversation—and such interruption and exposure will be generated by the particular experiences and presuppositions of both the interlocutor and Mabel. For me it was a story about people Mabel and I know, people from our community. For someone else it may have been Mabel's response "calamine lotion" to a question about Indians and poison oak.

Of course, interlocutors will not necessarily see themselves as exposed. They may have a completely different interpretation of the situation; Mabel can be seen as odd, crazy, or intentionally obscure to the extent that she is, in the words of my undergraduate professor, "impossible to crack." Then again her interlocutors may be confused or intimidated and for any number of reasons choose not to explore what is perplexing. In these situations the possibility of dialogue that is interruptive is foreclosed. Mabel may stop her interlocutors without challenging them. If some element of the speech event is interruptive within the larger exchange between Mabel and the interlocutors, it can be seen in two interdependent arenas: in that place where the point of exposure occurs and within the interlocutor's "inner dialogue" such that her words and ideas become "internally persuasive." This internal activity can continue after the initial interruption.

For days I kept thinking about the girls and their mother. I drove to the little clapboard house at the south end of town where I remembered waiting with a group of friends for the girls to give us a sign that their mother had gone up the street to play cards. The family had long since moved—they had moved several times, living here and there on the fringes of town like many Indian families I knew. The house was painted another color, not the dull off-white I remembered but a bright yellow with sepia trim. I thought of other "strange stories" I heard while growing up.

Back in college, after my visit home, I had a sense of why descriptions and discussions of American Indians felt so incomplete. As Mabel would say, "there is more to the story." Any discussion of shamanism, for instance, brought to mind this entire story, not just how the girls' grandmother was poisoned by a poisoning shaman but about how my own experiences met with those of the family in the story. And this sense that there is more to the story makes me think of something else I feel is missing in the studies of American Indians, indeed in the studies of other cultures in general—not the kinds of personal contact I have had, not even a brief acquaintance with a person from another culture, although any of these things can be helpful, but interruption and risk. How do scholars see beyond the norms they use to frame the experiences of others unless those norms are interrupted and exposed so that scholars are vulnerable, seeing what they think as possibly wrong, or at least limited?

Of course the story does not end, as I discovered one day while Mabel and I were driving up near Clear Lake looking at the various places she remembered as a young woman. We came upon a tract of land just above the lake, near Sulfur Bank, where the woman in the story had been poisoned. Parked alongside the road, gazing at an open lot between two newish ranch style homes, Mabel began to speak:

"See a priest gave the Indian people this land to live on. They had no place to go during that time, them who was around here down by Sulfur Bank. He let them live here, the priest. See _____'s husband, he was from this place."

"She wasn't?"

"No, she was from the valley, over the mountains there. When they [_____'s people] got moved from that place they got split up. Soldiers—white people—marched them to Covelo. Some went to Ukiah. Her father, he went to Santa Rosa, I believe. She come here to this place and married that man.

"See I had a man here too. When they give me in marriage first time. Them girls [mother and aunts of the girls I know] was small yet. Then I left, when I was over with that man. I went back to Rumsey. I never saw but I heard what happened—how that man poisoned. Then I never seen _____ until that day at the laundromat, in Santa Rosa.

"Well, I always stick up for her though. She was born there and her mother is the one took Grandma in dancing there after Grandma and then got put off the old place on Cache Creek. Took Grandma in dancing. Adopted Grandma in up there when she had nowhere to go. So that's how I call _____ cousin."

The story opened onto a broader, historic context. The earlier stages of European colonization affected, directly and indirectly, the lives of the women in the story and Mabel. I mentioned this idea, and Mabel retorted: "Yes, them days was hard time. Killing. Raping time, how they [Europeans] done with the women. Starvation. People moving . . . You know about people moving around, different people."

I took these last words as a direct statement about my life, about my living in different homes as I was growing up. In that way I had a small sense, on a personal level, of the displacement our ancestors experienced. And the same history plays itself out in the present with so many I know. Witness the family about whom the story was told. Witness the fact that eighty percent of California Indian school children drop out of school by ninth grade, and that the life expectancy is forty-seven years and suicide for teenage Indian males is ten times the state average for that age group. To gather materials to make the baskets art historians and basket specialists admire so, Mabel must search roadside ditches or ask permission to enter private property where her ancestors in large numbers gathered freely to dig sedge root and cut willow and redbud. Clearly, for Mabel a discussion about the material aspects of her basketry cannot be separated from a discussion of other things, history among them. And this history was not only something which my life experience helped me to understand; it also played an integral role in the constitution of my experience and mixed heritage.

If Mabel's talk initiates in the interlocutors a kind of internal dialogue where the interlocutors examine the nature of their own thinking, that dialogue can be carried over to an ever-widening context of talk in stories and conversations. Thus a simultaneous opening of two worlds continues. The shorter pieces of dialogue I related, mostly responses to questions, illustrate various points where interruptive dialogue can begin. The story I told shows how it can continue.

Some might suggest that I have been positioned as an initiate learning the rules of entry into another worldview or society. Stories and conversations may open and overlap, thus evoking themes or morals, but my understanding of them will always be tied to my larger experience. I cannot reconstruct Mabel's world independent of my experience of it. The dynamic of her talk undermines the authority I would have to assume to do so. What I can do is reconstruct my relationship to her world, at least to the extent I understand it at this time, and this essay has been just such an attempt. Mabel is not a pedant; her talk is improvisational, emergent, always pointing beyond itself such that it is difficult to see what she says as representing one thing or another. Even as a place or name might suggest certain things (i.e., taboo, a historic occurrence), other talk—a new story or topic of conversation—can affect meaning as the listener has previously constructed it. So while the talk may evoke certain themes and morals, these are presented such that they become themes and morals for a generative understanding of the worlds Mabel and I share. She is not Don Juan and I am not Carlos

Castaneda; neither is her talk a drug that plunks me into a separate reality.

Of course, as I have mentioned, my position is unique, as is anyone's, but if my familiarity with aspects of Mabel's world—I am thinking particularly of my knowledge of people and places she talks about—affects anything, it is the texture and not the dynamic of the talk. I refer to Toelken's notion of texture "as any coloration given a traditional Item or statement as it is being made." Of course how one determines what is "traditional" is problematic, especially when you consider that Mabel is speaking English. (If Mabel were speaking to someone in Cache Creek Pomo, more than texture might be affected, perhaps even the dynamic of the talk as I have been discussing it. I do not speak Cache Creek Pomo and neither does anyone else.) My familiarity with certain people and places allows Mabel to invoke by allusion the setting of a story or the thematization of an idea, whereas with others who are not familiar with these people and places, through either personal association or other talk, she would have to spell things out. The mere mention of a feature in the landscape, for instance, may bring to mind a story and a notion of taboo associated with the feature. Keith Basso observes that among the Western Apache "geographical features have served for centuries as mnemonic pegs on which to hang the moral teachings of their history," that "narrative events are 'spatially anchored' at points on the land, and that the evocative pictures presented by Western Apache place-names become indispensable resources for the storyteller's craft." This familiarity is not unusual for a community that has shared over millennia the same landscape and various stories associated with the landscape, and often accounts for the paucity of natural description and human motivation typically found in the literature of such a community. But in my case, familiarity with a landscape and certain people cannot presume an understanding of the landscape and people, at least not in Mabel's terms. While I might know some things and continue to learn, the dynamic of the talk remains the same.

Certainly Mabel's life has been unique in many ways. As mentioned, only six members of the Cache Creek Pomo were living when she was born, and though she was raised by her maternal grandmother, Sarah Taylor, she was not raised on or near Lolsel, the main Long Valley Cache Creek village at the time of European contact. She grew up among the southwestern Wintun in the Rumsey area of the Sacramento Valley, where Sarah had gone to find work. She traveled with a carnival for a while, dancing the Charleston every night before large crowds; in San Francisco she worked as a maid for the madam of one of the better known houses of ill repute. She tells stories about these aspects of her life. Her experiences as a contemporary American Indian woman are many, and her personal history is complex, varied, multicultural. But it must be remembered, underlined here, that Mabel has never presented herself as a representative of one thing or another. She fights typification; she rebukes the attempts of those who wish to see her in an ahistorical light, as merely a vestige of a prelapsarian world.

And it is in this struggle that her talk interferes with any move that would displace history from myth or from any number of things she talks about. A story may be beautiful in and of itself, but it is not timeless. The interlocutor's experience is not displaced either; it is held up, and therefore affirmed, juxtaposed not to show how one experience or worldview is better than the other but to expose the tension between them.

Tedlock suggests that "anthropological dialogue creates a world, or understanding of the differences between two worlds, that exists between persons who were indeterminately far apart, in all sorts of different ways, when they started out on their conversation." This betweenness can become the locus of cultural critique whose aim, as Marcus and Fischer say, is "not the statement and assertion of values [but] the empirical exploration of the historical and cultural conditions for the articulation and implementation of different values." One contemporary technique for cultural critique is a "strategy of defamiliarization" where "disruption of common sense, doing the unexpected, placing familiar subjects in unfamiliar, or even shocking, contexts are the aims of this strategy to make the reader [or listener] conscious of difference." This betweenness, if jarring to some extent, can expose and challenge presuppositions predicated on cultural and historic conditions that shape the way(s) people think about themselves and others. Mabel's talk provides her interlocutors this opportunity to see the constructedness of their own culture and history as they are confronted by what in her world does not make sense. If Mabel McKay is the last of her tribe, indeed the last of many roles among the Pomo people, she is not simply going to describe what was; she is going to invoke the present that accounts for what is.

Dialogue is essential here, dialogue that interrupts and disrupts preconceived notions, that can open the intermingling of the multiple voices and histories within and between people. To some extent Mabel assumes a teacher's role in the speech activity. She disrupts the kind of dialogue that has been typical between fieldworkers and informants. Yet it must be remembered that the dialogue with Mabel is not necessarily meant to teach a specific rule or idea but to expose something about the relationship between Mabel and her interlocutors and how that is affecting their understanding of one another.

Some of the newer ethnographic endeavors and textual recreations of oral literature seek to reveal, among other things, the different worldviews and interactions among participants—field-workers and native scholars—and the problems that arise as a result. Difficulties are likely to surface with the textualizing process and should be made apparent to the reader. Responding to the call for polyvocality, these texts present multiple voices and narrative forms. They are said to be collaborative in nature. For Mabel McKay and her interlocutors, talk itself initiates and sets the groundwork for collaboration. It is an art generating respect for the unknown while illuminating the borders of the known.

What I have written in this essay immediately reminds me of a story. The context of this storytelling event I do not remember, except that Mabel and I were driving, looking at old places Mabel remembered as a child.

"Do you know how babies are born?" she asked.

Of course I knew the facts of life. Mabel had something else on her mind.

"Like this," she said. "The spirit follows the parents for two years before it is born. It follows, watching. It knows everything. Even when it is born it knows everything.

"Until it starts walking, talking. Maybe a year old. Then it forgets, falls apart what it knows.

"Then, you know, it starts learning again. If the person gets old, REAL old, it will be all together again. In between is what you call living."

AUTHOR'S NOTE: Mabel McKay passed away on May 31, 1993.

Louise Bernice Halfe

Blue Marrow

"*Blue Marrow* is a book of . . . characters. Grandmothers both actual and spiritual . . . but many other people, past and present, also appear: Native men and women, fur traders, Jesuits, Metis, all of whose stories interact . . ."

❁

Adeline Cardinal, Emma Woods, Sara Cardinal, Bella Shirt, Nancy Gladue, Fanny Sunchild, Round Face Woman, Charlotte, *Ah-gat,* Bernard Woman, Pray to them.

My Grandfather *Wēpēmēs*, and his wife *Wāpasōs*, Frying Pan Woman, First Rays of Dawn Woman, Vera, Pauline Johnson, Waskewitch Woman, Wet Pants Woman, Carter Woman, Rubber Mouth Woman, Louiza. Pray to them.

Ehanh (Sarcee Woman), Lightning Woman, McGuiness Woman, One Spot Woman . . .

Grandmothers hold me. I must pass all that I possess, every morsel
to my children. These small gifts to see them through life. Raise my
fist. Tell the story. Tear down barbed-wire fences.

I wrote His Emminence,
offered my life to save savage souls.

My mother kissed my crucifix,
said, God go with you.

I am filled with wind, empty forest,
savages peck beneath my robe,
tender hands send heat up my spine.
I bless them.

This whip doesn't bite hard enough, Mother.
I crouch under the cross. Shroud my face.
Swallow. Swallow. Swallow.

This salt water I trickle,
send Father's Bible thundering.
God be with you.

Oh little one,
I've become a gopher,
jumping hole to hole,
arms too weak to bury
my crusted babies.
My heart a gooseberry
rolling my tongue.
I have gone with a man
who has a wooden tail,
a grunting guttural grizzly
eats my breast.
I am parched gra ˚
wetting my thi t.
My father's wails long,
buried.
E-pēcimakik.
I haunt them.
My wailing stories.

When the Voices roar,
I write.
Sometimes they sing,
are silent.
In those times
I read, answer overdue letters,
go for a walk or jog,
stoke my fire, prepare baloney
mustard sandwich, wild rice salad.
I haunt them.
My wailing stories.

❀

Everydime we turn a corner 'round dem lakes da land stop my
breathing. Over each hill we climb, god's hand stretch more dan our
eye can see. Old Womens' Lake, Where the Moose Died, Dried
Meat Hills. I pull my rosary an dank da god for dem sky an hills.
Swear da devil when we suffer from wads of mosquito, noseeums,
horseflies. Somedime go hungry for days. Plenty animal but our
hunters waz clomping trough dem woods scare da by jesus outta da
moose. Da savages waz good to us. Dress in dem furs an leather,
faces paint. Not one fat savage, dough can't say anyone of us waz
ever in lard. I see many change in my dime.

Sing. Sing, *Nōhkomak.*
Lend me your wind.
Over the prairie
her Voice rolled.

aiy aiy aiy Nōsisim
here this needle
thread its eye
oh these stories so small
pull them out
squeeze them through
aiy aiy aiy Nōsisim
some song come tumbling out
weak and small
aiy aiy aiy Nōsisim
we will dance
your fingers
stitch this cloth
mend these moccasins
light my Pipe
aiy aiy aiy Nōsisim
so long we've sat
aiy aiy aiy Nōsisim
we've waited for so long

VISIT TEEPEE TOWN

They hobbled, limped, shuffled,
pink, purple, blues, reds, yellows
white, black, printed blazed dresses,
shawls, kerchiefs, blankets.
Dried flowers, old sweat
and sweet perfume, they teased,
laughed, joked and gossiped.
Ran their fingers through each
swinging hand. Pipe smoke
swirled. Men drumming our songs.

I watch them. Hundreds of my husband's family.
They've traveled across Canada, the United States,
rejoice at recognizing one another,
some for the first time.
Each has brought a book they've lovingly compiled.
It contains the history of their migration
from England, Norway and into the Dakotas.
They are scattered throughout Turtle Island.
They marvel at the trek of their ancestors.
The click of wine glasses echoes through the arbour
of this large family gathering. And five Indians.
I the eldest, my children and two other Indian youths.
They are not yet aware how this affects their lives.

How many of relatives were cattled
onto the reservation during their settlement? How
much of my people's blood was spilled for this
migration? Laughter and wonder
as fingers move across the atlas. This where
great-granddad Arne crossed on the barge.
This is where great-great-granddad traveled
and preached the law of the land and where his
wife Isobel taught the little savages to read.
My lips are tight from stretching when my
small family is introduced alongside the
large extended family. Later, driving home,
I weave a story for my children—how their
great-grandma rode sidesaddle, waving
her .22 in the air trying to scare those relatives
away. I tell them how my relatives lived
around the fort, starving and freezing,
waiting for diluted spirits and handouts
from my husband's family. I tell them
how my little children died wrapped
in smallpox blankets. My breath
won't come anymore
I stare at the wheat fields.

I want to kick doze jesus out, boot you fudder in da ass,
his face fallin' to da floor an creep da night.
I want to dake da rifle an shoot
doze jesus out, you fudder, we went to boarding scold
but him he laid down his moudth
an only poured da spirts in.
When he dought dat udder man
douch my spoon his boot an fist come fly,
even dought da jesus spend his dime dere.

Kikisisin cī? *Do you 'member*
da ācimowina *about* Wēsākēcāhk? *I dold you dat story*
dat night. Even dough you didn't no what doze jesus
said, you eyes no dat look of ugly spirit in you fudder's eye.
You ears no dat story of woman hide in bush. No place to hide
I rub you belly sleep, burn large wood, our cabin durned cold.
In bed I rub my fingers into da dirt, wet da mud deep
in my pillow I die dat night.

❀

Did our Grandmothers know we would be scarred by the fists and
boots of men? Our songs taxed, silenced by tongues that speak
damnation and burning? Did they know we would turn woman
against woman? Did they know some of us would follow, take mates
of colour and how the boarding of our world would pulse breathing
exiles connected to their womb? Did they know only some would
dig roots, few hands calloused from tanning? Did they know only a
few would know the preparation of moose nose, gopher, beaver-tail
feasts? Did they know our memory, our talk would walk on paper,
legends told sparingly? Did they know of our struggling hearts?

Native Writings After the Detours

Peter Blue Cloud

Coyote's Discourse on Power, Medicine, and Would-be Shamans

Good evening, friends. You notice this long, straight branch I'm carrying? It's called a ten foot pole. It's best used to approach certain subjects which don't like to be approached. Then, if the subject snaps at you to bite your head off, or your heart out, with a bit of luck it'll bite the pole first and you can run away.

You see this old hat I'm wearing? It smells kind of funky, but it keeps the sun out of my eyes and the rain out of my hair. It also holds my head together, which is why I never take it off. By holding my head together, my brains stay intact. And you'll also, I hope, notice the holes in my hat from which my ears protrude? These ears, of course, are my sensors, used to detect sounds which immediately are fed to my brain for diagnostic purposes, for clarification, if you will. You will also note that my mouth is situated slightly below my ears and brain; and the other object of interest, my heart, is even further removed from the others. When functioning. The progression is from ear to mind to heart, then back to mind to be either stored away for later reference, or from mind to mouth to express an opinion on the information received.

Of course this isn't to say that the other parts of the body are not also vital, for they are, each necessary to the other. Like all things within the Creation, the loss of one causes an imbalance within the whole.

Take an asshole, for instance, that puckered, smirking thing we coyotes refer to as "the other mouth." The upper mouth takes in nourishment and also spew-out words, often incomprehensible. But the lower one knows enough to do only its job, which is getting rid of waste material, or compost, to put it better.

Speaking of assholes, I knew a young fellow once, about one-tenth as smart as he claimed to be. Lost his asshole one time because he forgot to listen. He was out gathering mushrooms when one of them spoke to him and said, "Don't pick me. I am a medicine!" He immediately plucked the mushroom from the ground and popped it into his mouth: figured, hell, if this is medicine maybe it'll do something wonderful and strange for me. (For of course this young fellow was never happy or healthy, being always too busy telling others how to live to take the time to take care of himself). Well, he got really sick. Vomited, farted and shit all over himself. Shit so much, in fact, that his asshole fell off without him even knowing it. Probably still running around looking for it. Yes, he's the first person I ever met with a detachable asshole.

Anyway, I'm here tonight to speak of medicine and those some call shamans. I need the money you're paying to hear about these subjects. So, okay, I just mentioned both in one sentence and that's probably a beginning.

And now I want to tell you about a young woman I met on a famous university campus. Met her at a party. She walked right up to me and started looking at me thru a crystal. She looked and looked, then told me very seriously: "I'm a medicine woman, you know. You must come and see me." I kept a very serious look on my own face and told her solemnly, "Yes, I will come to see you. What is your name and address?" "Oh," she said, hesitating momentarily, "Shamaness Fast-Walker. Meet me by that big oak up the hill. Right after the party." Then she walked away to crystal a few others.

She was pretty good-looking, so I went and met her later. Asked her to put her pouch of crystals behind the oak, then we got down to the business of the two-backed dance and other forms of strenuous frivolity. After our final performance, which was a take-off on aerial acrobatics done hanging from an oak branch, she retrieved her crystals and proceeded to "do me," as she called it. It was a full moon night. The stars glittered and danced within the crystal.

I'd learned very young to counteract powers I had not requested. I stared back at her through the crystal. She began fading. I could see the moon thru her body. Her eyes dimmed and her mouth opened to plead with me. But it was too late. I couldn't stop myself. She faded completely away, not even leaving the trace of a shadow.

Someday I'll bring her back. She did know some good tricks, though they had more to do with body magic.

I went to another party on the same campus, given to celebrate the arrival of a well-known poet. His fame was based on the fact that he was, quote: "A Shaman Poet!" unquote. Now, that's really heavy, I thought, settling down with the others to hear his poems. He began chanting his poems in a deep, slow voice. Every other line spoke of his powers to understand all things within the Creation. His choruses called on his powers to hear him, to reaffirm these powers.

He was beautiful, his long hair swaying in rhythm to his body movements, his white-streaked beard jutting-out in profound wisdom. I was very impressed. I looked around at the others and saw that they were as if in a trance. His words and motions had acted to put everyone under his spell. Oh, he had power all right, real magnetism.

I reached for him with my mind, to share some of that strength. I touched a shell and put my ear to it. I heard the echoes of his own words bouncing back and forth within a hollow shell. Then I probed his mind. I went inside of it to find a tight bundle of self, a bursting ball of energy looking out of eyes which were intent only on seducing his audience.

I felt sad. I withdrew and sat with the others. I'd stopped listening, for I was depressed. Here is no shaman, I thought, here is a powerful mind centered on self.

Being a creature native to this continent, I'm often accused of siding with my indigenous relatives. I deny this and will state at this time that power and wisdom are universal. No one center of this earth possesses the allness of power. I would also like to say at this time that phonies, too, are universal. But then perhaps, like decay, the phonies are necessary compost to the growth of real power. But who can know?

Take a drum and a rattle. Take a people sitting in circle around a fire, singing songs of the Creation. The very same songs their ancestors sang.

Now take the same people and let a flea of dissatisfaction bite one of them. A young man (let's pick on him) takes the drum passed to him by an elder. Even before he consents to begin drumming, he must first change the painted designs on the drum. Then he removes the feathers and replaces them with bells. Now he's ready. He begins the ancient beat, then hesitates. It is too slow. So he speeds up the beat to satisfy and keep pace with his quick mind. The song is new. The people listen respectfully, seeking to share a newness. But the young man is still not satisfied, and before the people can begin to comprehend his song, he has begun another. Then quickly he does variations on the theme until the theme itself has been lost, swallowed-up in his frenzy. Even he has forgotten the original theme. "Well," he says, in explanation, "That's progress!"

Sort of reminds me of a pup when it's agitated for some reason and begins chasing and biting at its own tail. That's what's called "a tight circle of concentration."

Where was I? Seems like I'm going in circles myself, don't it? Do I seem bitter or anything? I hope not, after all, I want you to invite me back.

Yes, well, the first time it happened was so long ago that even I barely remember. It was a girl child out walking thru the forest alone. But not alone, because the little people were curious and followed her. She was out walking because she felt bad. Her father had been hurt while hunting. He'd cut open his leg on a branch sticking from a tree at ground level. He'd been too eager, he admitted to his family. Game was scarce and he was trying too hard and had forgotten caution. It was his own fault, he insisted. And now the cut was swollen with puss and would not heal.

And so the little girl was walking, trying to keep herself from crying. Tears were not much of a cure for physical pain, she knew. The little people sensed her great sorrow and decided to let her see them. They wanted to know why she was feeling such sorrow.

They let themselves be seen by her. She'd always known they lived in these woods, but this was the first time she'd seen them. They were all very formal as they introduced themselves. They liked her very much and felt a deep respect for her sorrow.

Asking politely the source of her sorrow, after they got to know her, she told them all. The little people sat with her in silence for a long time. Finally, one of them spoke softly, telling the girl to continue her walk, and to pay close attention to everything she passed.

The girl continued on into the forest, watching and listening. In a clearing, as she stepped across a small brook, she heard a tiny, polite cough. She looked all around, but couldn't find the source. Then the cough was repeated and she looked down. There, right next to her, a small green plant was nodding and moving its leaves.

There being no breeze and it being the only thing around in motion, the child knelt to study the plant.

It spoke to her then, apologizing for coughing and interrupting her walk. The plant explained that the little people had asked it to help her. It then told her that it possessed a power of curing. It would teach the girl its powers if she would take the time to learn how to use it properly. The process was involved, but was soon learned by the girl. It included a cleansing, a chant, a song, a slow process of preparation, a further singing to be shared by the person being cured, and this was to be followed by a thank-you feast for the Creation. The plant emphasized that the thank-you not be made to the plant itself, but to all things within the Creation.

The child picked the plant and some of its relatives as instructed and returned home. She told her family of the gift she'd been given, and then prepared the cure. Her father was cured so quickly that he was able to go out and hunt the very food which was used for the thank-you feast.

The girl child grew to maturity and became known as a curing person. She always followed the first instructions given by the plant, step by step slowly, so that she made no mistake. As she grew in mind and body, so too grew her knowledge of medicine, for the little people never ceased to talk to her even in her old age. And as time passed, she was given to know many other curing plants, one by one as they were needed.

She shared her knowledge with a few others, so that it would stay alive within her tribe. Not everyone is given the patience to learn the curing arts. Many other skills are needed within a tribe to assure survival. Usually, as a person grows, their own particular skills will manifest themselves. As with everything else, when all the arts and skills are combined, a strong unity exists within the tribe.

And with all this I'd like to add that I've never yet met a person of power (except himself, of course) who gives themselves titles such as medicine person, power person, or shaman. Even within a tribe or nation, the people know who to see for their particular needs, so why give them titles?

When porcupine goes night walking, he doesn't look behind himself and say, "Ah, yes, I got my quills with me." He knows what he's got.

Well, my friends, that's about it for this time. As you leave you may notice a little basket sitting by the door. It's called a hunger basket, and if you would be kind enough to feed it a little money, it will be a very happy basket.

Thank you.

Coyote's Anthro

The anthropologist was very excited. He'd just received his doctorate after having delivered his paper, entitled: The Mythology of Coyote: Trickster, Thief, Fool and World-Maker's Helper. He was at this very moment in the process of gathering further data, working on a generous grant from a well-known Foundation. He'd just setup camp in the sagebrush not far from his latest informant's shack.

Now he sat by his fire, looking at the stars and sipping coffee. He chuckled to himself when he heard a coyote bark not far away. He wondered what that coyote would think if the myths about him (or her) were read aloud?

"Not much!" Said a voice. The anthro was startled, he hadn't heard anyone approach. "Not much, maybe just a cup of coffee and some of that cake I see sitting there." Then into the campfire light stepped an old man, but not a man. He had long, furry ears sticking thru his felt hat, and he had a long, bushy tail hanging from beneath his greatcoat. He leaned on his walking stick and grinned.

Good God! The anthro was stunned: it was Coyote Old Man himself. But it couldn't be; he was a myth!

"Not always." Coyote said, as the anthro closed his eyes and shook his head violently from side to side. When he opened his eyes, Coyote was leaning toward him, his head cocked sideways, listening. He nodded, "Yes, I heard them there in your head. Sounded like pebbles. Is that how you anthro's make music?"

The anthro knew he must be hallucinating. Better go along with it, he thought frantically, and maybe it'll go away. "Uh, are you Coyote Old Man?" He asked.

"Do I look like Fox Young Man? And do you really want me to go away?" Coyote studied the anthro, then asked, "What time are you?"

The anthro raised his arm to look at his watch, "Well, it's exactly . . . "

Coyote interrupted. "Nothing's exactly. It's not tick-tock time I asked about. I just want to know what time you are." The anthro looked blank. "I thought so," said Coyote, "Well, let's have that coffee, then we can maybe figure things out."

So they sat drinking coffee, the anthro so excited he couldn't sit still. He reached for his tape recorder, then looked at Coyote, "Uh, do you mind if I turn this on?"

"Why not? Do you pet it or sing to it? Will it dance?"

Once he'd turned on his tape recorder, he felt more confident. He was, after all, an anthropologist: He picked up his note book and pencil, and began, "I'll pay you for your time, of course," he said.

"It's not really mine I'm worried about, it's yours I'm here for. How can you pay me for my time when you don't know what your own is? How about this time? Yes, this time put a little more sugar in my coffee." Coyote laughed at himself, then looked seriously at the anthro; "I'm a doctor, you know. I'm here to help you. Now then, how can I help you?"

"Well, actually, it's the stories I'm most concerned with. The reasons behind the reasons, if you follow me: interrelationships, the problem of special paradox, sexual taboos, those kinds of things. I want to creat a whole fabric of thought, a completed tapestry, no loose threads. Know what I mean?"

"Parrot Boxes, huh? Sex shell tables and followyouse: what's all that? That how you talk about pussy in college? You know, you sound like my tapeworm, and he never did make any sense. How about just one question to begin with, huh?"

"Well, let's start with the Creation myth, cutting to the core! What's the meat of it really, the true meaning?"

"My friend," said Coyote, "If you think Creation's a myth, you just might be in serious trouble. It's not the learning that's important, but the leaning. You must lean toward your questions, your problems; lean slowly so that you don't bend the solution too badly out of shape."

Coyote plucked a long hair from his tail and held it horizontally a foot from the ground. He whispered something to the hair, then let it go, and it floated there where he'd held it. He took a sip of coffee, then placed his cup on the hair. The anthro was incredulous: the cup sat on the hair above the ground. He blurted out, "But how did you do that? What's holding the hair up?"

You're not studying your notes to this story very well, are you? If you'll just relook at the paragraph in front of this one you'll find that a foot from the ground is holding things up. Of course, you can't see the foot 'cause I just made-up its measured guess. Something invisible is sleeping under this sand and only its foot is sticking out."

And so, because this story is getting too long, Coyote became somewhat impatient, and quickly finished his coffee. He stood up and beckoned the anthro, "Come on then, we got some leaning to do." And Coyote led him across the desert to a deep pool of water near some mountains.

A full moon was reflected in the water, shining as brightly as the one in the sky. Coyote sat down and began singing. Then, still softly singing, he leaned out over the water and touched the reflected moon. The water bent to his touch like rubber. Still singing he stepped onto the water moon, bouncing slightly. He jumped a bit and bounced up and down.

Then he began bouncing in earnest, bounding into the sky, even doing a couple of back flips. He bounced as high as he could and grabbed the moon in the sky and hung there grinning at the anthro. "Hey, look at me," he said, "and I wasn't even sure I could do it."

He let go of the moon, did a double flip, bounced once and landed next to the anthro. "Okay," he said, "I got it all nice and rubbery. Go ahead and bounce a little."

So the anthro jumped from the bank, creating a great splash as he sank from view. He was gasping and spitting out water as he climbed from the pool.

"Well, well, look how you shattered the moon . . . You know, I thought only us coyotes were silly enough to try things we weren't sure of. And you, my friend, forgot to sing."

The Other Side of Nowhere: Twenty Poet Sketches

1

The Gourmet Poet breaks
bread with fat fingers.
never forgetting to leave
a few crumbs for the hungry.
He sips only the best of wines
and delicately licks the juices
of roast beef from his fingers.
He usually dines at a one-table
sidewalk cafe he had built
in front of his tenement.
The neighbors tend to ignore him
as he snaps his fingers
at imaginary waiters
and compliments to the chef.

2

The Landscape Poet met
herself half way round
a circular composition.
Since neither would give way
or retreat they decided to
adopt one another
and became twins.

3

      The Doubting Poet spends
so much of his time
wondering if he should
be more sure of himself,
that he no longer composes
anything, let alone
      himself.

4

      The Classics Poet was
finally discovered
by a research student
in the archives of
the university library.
quite mummified
except for a halo
radiating like
      blurred footnotes

5

Another Poet I always
forget to mention
suffers this fate frequently,
and so it is that no one
    knows his name.

6

The Creative Poet who was trapped
in the upper left hand corner
of the paper he was working on
quickly wrote his name
and folded himself into
that corner, and a lot of people
    are still searching for him.

7

The Rock Star Poet does
his thing on the backsides
of his personal groupies
with a diamond needle.
After each poetic incision
he'll usually say,
"Why don't you, ah,
    sit on it awhile?"

8

    The x-Rated Poet lives
in a woodshed lined
with literary criticisms of
his most notorious works,
basing all his concepts
of sin upon
        their contents.

9

    The Doom Poet was
forever catching tigers
by their tails, only
to have them
burst into flame, trying
in their own fashion
to give him a little
        enlightenment.

10

    The Enlightened Poet who
levitated above his station
was quickly brought to earth
by a sharp ego-jab
administered by
       his jealous Guru.

11

    The Jealous Guru Poet who
couldn't walk on water
settled far out on a desert.
One day he was caught up
by a flashflood and
deposited as sediment for
       future speculation.

12

    A Women's Lib Poet I met
at a cocktail party
challenged me to a composition
and together we did
       a somewhat sweaty piece.

13

The Chauvinist Poet
was quite upset at
being called just that
but he felt much better
when his grandmother
assured him
that chauvinists
often became
great wizards.

14

The Marijuana Poet
coughs and wheezes
his way along
intricate patterns
only he
can see.

15

    The Lesser Poet who
lived on the tenth floor
of a somewhat rundown tenement
would stand at his open window
and recite his verses
to the people far below.
A crowd would always gather
which pleased him immensely
for he loved a decent audience.
"Do you think he'll jump?"
A fat lady asked, unpacking
another sandwich.
"If he does, I hope he waits
awhile," said a local politician
unfolding a soapbox and
        tuning-up his bullhorn.

16

    The Scavenger Poet wheeled in
a battered baby buggy in which
lay an ugly little troll.
He shook the creature awake
and turned to me smirking:
"Well, what do you think of it?"
I was at a loss for words,
of course, and he impatiently
declared, "Wouldn't you know it,
nothing to say. And to think,
I just wrote this baby
        this morning."

17
      The Vegetarian Poet who
resembles a grain elevator
was attacked by a swarm
of hungry yellowjackets.
"If this is a meat substitute:"
one of them buzzed
"I hope his poetry has
        more juice."

18
      The Poet of Standing when
finally offered a seat
at a famous university
was heard to mumble
"Well, I guess I may
as well
        sit the next one out."

19
     The Sarcastic Poet was
reciting his latest work
to the consternation
of an empty room,
when suddenly
and for the fifth
time that day:
          nothing happened.

               20
               The Aerodynamic Poet
          whizzes in and around
          and about and above
          so swiftly that
          he seldom has time
          to join us for
               a quick one.

contributors

JAMES THOMAS STEVENS (ARONHIÓTAS) is an enrolled member of the Akwesasne Mohawk Tribe. He was born to a Welsh father and Mohawk mother in Niagara Falls, New York in 1966. Stevens attended the Institute of American Indian Arts in Santa Fe, New Mexico and received a full fellowship to attend Brown University's graduate writing program, where he received his MFA in 1993. Stevens currently teaches English/Creative Writing at Haskell Indian Nations University in Lawrence, Kansas.

LISE MCCLOUD is the 1996 winner of Minnesota Monthly's Tamarack Award for fiction. Her work has been published in journals and anthologies including *Aboriginal Voices, Cream City Review, NDQ, Prairie Volcano, Sing Heavenly Muse!, Tamaqua, Two Worlds Walking,* and *XCP.*

GERALD VIZENOR is a professor of Native American Literature and American Studies at the University of California/Berkeley. He is the author of more than twenty books on native histories, literature, and critical studies, including *The People Named The Chippewa* and *Manifest Manners.* His most recent books are *Hotline Healers: an Almost Browne Novel,* and *Fugitive Poses: Native American Indian Scenes of Absence and Presence.* Vizenor is series editor of American Indian Literature and Critical Studies at the University of Oklahoma Press.

JAMES LUNA is included in *The Sound of Rattles and Clappers:* A collection of New California Indian Writing. He lives on the La Jolla Reservation in North County San Diego, California.

ROSMARIE WALDROP's most recent books include *Another Language: Selected Poems, A Key Into the Language of America,* and *Lawn of Excluded*

Middle. She is co-publisher with Keith Waldrop of Burning Deck Press in Providence, Rhode Island. She is also a well-known translator, having worked on books by Edmond Jabès and Paul Celan.

MARIE ANNHARTE BAKER b. Winnepeg, Manitoba, Canada. Her poetry includes the books *Being on the Moon* and *Coyote Columbus Café*. Baker is a student, cybergranny (Nat Lit), and the stand-up routine performer of "Granny Boot Camp." She is currently working on the multimedia project "Commie Conversations on Commercial Drive."

CAROLYN LEI-LANILAU is a poet, artist, and scholar who lives in Oakland, California and Honolulu Hawai'i. Her book *Wode shuofa (My Way of Speaking),* published under the name Carolyn Lau received a 1987 American Book Award for poetry. He most recent book is *Ono Ono Girl's Hula.*

BARBARA TEDLOCK is a Professor of Anthropology at the State University of New York at Buffalo. Her honors include appointment to the National Humanities Faculty; a Weatherhead Resident Fellowship at the School of American Research in Santa Fe; the Charles Borden, Geoffrey Bushnell, and Juan Comas Prize for the best paper in linguistics and the International Congress of Americanists; two NEH fellowships; and ACLS fellowship; and a visiting appointment at the Institute for Advanced Study at Princeton. She has published numerous articles and essays based on her extensive field research among the Zuni of New Mexico and the Maya of Guatemala and Belize. Her books are *Time and the Highland Maya, Teachings from the American Earth: Indian Religion and Philosophy* (with Dennis Tedlock); *Dreaming: Anthropological and Psychological Interpretations;* and *The Beautiful and the Dangerous: Dialogues with the Zuni Indians.* She has lectured on the Maya at the National Academy of Sciences in Washington and appeared on the NBC television special *Ancient Prophecies.* Having just completed a term as coeditor in chief of *The American Anthropologist,* she is currently at work on a book titled *The Woman in the Shaman's Body: Reclaiming the Feminine in Religion and Medicine.*

TJ SNOW is in the graduate program at the University of Calgary and is a member of the Nakoda Sioux First Nation. After curating and exhibiting at several sites, museums, and galleries, he is currently working on a creative thesis using image-text sculptural installation.

LINDA HOGAN is the author of several books including the poetry collection *Savings* and the novel *Mean Spirit*. Her work has received numerous awards including the Guggenheim, National Endowment for the Arts, and American Book Award. She teaches in the University of Colorado Creative Writing program.

WENDY ROSE Just turned fifty; full-time instructor in American Indian Studies at Fresno City College, Fresno, California; also co-owner of a science fiction/fantasy collectibles store called Oh Grow Up in Fresno; lives on the southern tip of the Mother Lode in the Sierra Nevada foothills near Coarsegold; has published thirteen books of poetry and appeared in nearly one hundred anthologies and periodicals since 1967. Most recent books are *Bone Dance* (Univ. of Arizona Press, 1993) and *Now Poof She Is Gone* (Firebrand Press, 1994); occupies a spot on Lilley Mountain overlooking the San Joaquin Valley with an imperialist tabby cat and he love slave, cactus, koi, and assorted reptiles; just celebrated entering the twenty-third year of marriage to Arthur Murata; has a growing collection of female superhero, supervillain, and goddess figurines and dolls; leads a secret life as a block of granite.

MAURICE KENNY has authored numerous books, which include: *Common Days; Between Two Rivers, Rain & Other Fictions;* and the forthcoming *In the Tune of the Present*. He has received many awards including the prestigious American Book Award for the collection *The Mama Poems*. Kenny lives in Saranac Lake in the high peaks region of the Adirondacks and is presently a visiting professor at SUNY/Potsdam.

HACHIVI EDGAR HEAP OF BIRDS received his MFA from the Tyler School of Art in Philadelphia. A native Oklahoman of Cheyenne-Arapaho heritage, Heap of Birds's creative work centers on Native American issues and those of indigenous peoples throughout the world. His art addresses culture, identity, and Native American history through both textual and nonverbal imagery, symbols, and signs.

ALLISON ADELLE HEDGE COKE teaches for Man Drudo Summer Arts Program, California State University System. She has co-edited two collections of Native American poetry and writing: *Voices of Thunder* and *It's Not Quiet Anymore*. Hedge Coke grew up in North Carolina, Canada, and on the Great Plains. She holds an MFA in creative writing from Vermont College, attended Naropa Institute, and has an AFA in writing from the Institute of American Indian Arts.

VICTORIA LENA MANYARROWS is Tsalagi/Eastern Cherokee, forty years old, and a member of the Native Writers Circle of the Americas and the Indigenous Women's Network. Her first book of poetry, *Songs from the Native Lands*, was published by Nopal Press in 1995. She currently resides in San Francisco.

BESMILR BRIGHAM was born in 1913 in Pace, Mississippi with Choctaw predecessors on both sides. She attended Mary Hardin-Baylor College in Texas and the New School for Social Research in New York City. In 1970 she was the recipient of a Discovery Award from the National Endowment for the Arts. While her writing, both prose and poetry, spans fifty years, she accomplished most of her publishing between 1969 and 1976. She is the author of *Agony Dance: Death of the Dancing Dolls* and *Heaved from the Earth*.

NORA MARKS DAUENHAUER AND RICHARD DAUENHAUER have spent the last two decades collecting, transcribing, and documenting the Tlinglit oral tradition. They live in Juneau, Alaska.

DIANE GLANCY is Associate Professor at Macalester College where she teaches Native American Literature and Creative Writing. She has received a National Endowment for the Arts grant, a National Endowment for the Humanities grant, an American Book Award, the Native American Prose Award and a Loft McKnight Fellowship. Her latest book, *Fuller Man*, a novel, and a collection of stories, *The Voice That Was in Travel*, are forthcoming from Moyer Bell and the University of Oklahoma Press.

PHIL YOUNG is of Cherokee and Scotch-Irish descent, born in Henryetta, Oklahoma in 1947. His widely exhibited paintings, drawings, and installations are often mixed media, exploring relationships between the vandalism of cultures and desecration of the land. Humor finds its way into the serious issues of authenticity/identity and historical/cultural stereotypes of Native Americans which he addresses. He was awarded a Joan Mitchell Foundation Grant in Painting and Sculpture. Currently he is Professor of Art and Hartwick College in Oneonta, New York, where he has resided since 1978. In spite of his upstate residence, he states that "the red clay of Oklahoma still runs in my veins."

LARRY EVERS AND FELIPA MOLINA's most recent books include *Wo'I Bwikam: Coyote Songs* and *Yaqui Deer Songs (Maso Bwikam): A Native American Poetry*, winner of the Chicago Folklore Prize. Larry Evers is professor of English at the University of Arizona. Felipe S. Molina is a Yaqui singer who has served as governor of Yoem Pueblo and as a member of the Pascua Tribal Council.

SHERMAN ALEXIE's latest poetry collection is *The Summer of Black Widows* and his latest novel is *Indian Killer*. A film, *Smoke Signals*, for which he wrote a script adapted from one of the short stories in his book *The Lone Ranger and Tonto Fistfight in Heaven*, has won rave reviews and large audiences.

Alexie's poems and stories have appeared very widely and he has read from his work in virtually every state as well as in several European countries. Among many awards, he has won a Lila Wallace-Reader's Digest Writer's Award, an American Book Award, and a Creative Writing Fellowship from the National Endowment for the Arts.

An enrolled Spokane/Coeur d'Alene Indian, Alexie was born on the Spokane reservation in Wellpinit, Washington. He is very active in the American Indian community and frequently gives workshops. He now lives in Seattle, with his wife and infant son.

JUAN FELIPE HERRERA Cross-Mojado Poet, West Coast Salsista, dream pagan, Toon theater dancer, Chiapas drifter, & Sub-Minister of Conga Word Jams, Juan Felipe Herrera teaches cultural studies, creative writing, and Chicano teatro at CSU/Fresno. He lives with performance poet Margarita Luna Robles. Forthcoming ouvres: *Laughing Out Loud, I Fly: Bilingual Poems for Children,* (Harper Collins) and *Cilantro Facials: The Big Book of Latina and Chicano Toons & Comedy* (Temple).

GREG SARRIS is a professor of English at UCLA. He is currently serving his second consecutive term as chairman of the Federated Coast Miwok Tribe. His most recent novel is *Watermelon Nights,* published by Hyperion.

LOUISE BERNICE HALFE was born in Two Hill, Alberta. She was raised on the Saddle Lake Indian Reserve and attended Blue Quills Residential School. Louise earned her Bachelor of Social Work from the University of Regina, a certificate in Drugs & Alcohol Counseling from Nechi Institute. During a six-year stay in Northern Saskatchewan, while attending satellite classes and commuting to the University of Saskatchewan, she kept a journal. As a result, her first book of poetry *Bear Bones & Feathers* evolved and was published by Coteau Books. *Bear Bones & Feathers* was short-listed for the Spirit of Saskatchewan Award, the First Book Award, and the Gerald Lambert Award. In 1996, the book won the Milton Acorn Award. Louise's work has appeared in various anthologies and magazines, notably the *Saskatchewan NeWest Review.* Her second book titled *Blue Marrow,* is a mixture of prose, poetry, and journal writing from voices of the past and was published by McClelland in 1998. Louise recently completed a two-week residency as the Markin-Flanagan Distinguished Writer in Calgary, Alberta. She is married and has two children, one of whom has made her a proud grandmother of two.

PETER BLUE CLOUD's books include *Elderberry Flute Song: Contemporary Coyote Tales, Clan of Many Nations: Selected Poems 1969 – 1994,* and *The Other Side of Nowhere,* and he has received an American Book Award. He is a Mohawk of the Turtle Clan.

acknowledgments

JAMES STEVENS: *Tōkinish* is reprinted with permission of James Thomas Stevens, © 1994. Published by First Intensity Press (Staten Island, NY), in conjunction with shuffaloff books (Toronto, Canada).

LISE McCLOUD: "Mixed American Pak" first appeared in *XCP: Cross-Cultural Poetics #1*. Reprinted by permission of the author.

GERALD VIZENOR: pp. 74 – 76 of *Manifest Manners: Postindian Warriors of Survivance* © 1994 by Gerald Vizenor, Wesleyan University Press, by permission of University Press of New England. "Museum Bound" used by permission of the author. "Beavers" is reprinted from *Dead Voices: Natural Agonies in the New World* by Gerald Vizenor, pp. 100 – 115, reprinted by permission of the University of Oklahoma Press.

JAMES LUNA: Printed by permission of the artist. All art is copyright protected.

ROSMARIE WALDROP: Parts I, VI, VIII, XII, XIX, XXII, and XXIX reprinted from *A Key Into the Language of America* © 1994 by Rosmarie Waldrop. Reprinted by permission of New Directions Publishing Corp.

MARIE ANNHARTE BAKER: "One Appropriate First," "'Rangutan Rage Writes About Story," and "Beware Writer" originally appeared in West Coast Line #24. Reprinted by permission of the author.

CAROLYN LEI-LANILAU: "Hawaiians, no Kanaka, nah Hahh-Y-in" and "Ha'ina 'ia mai ana ka puana" reprinted from *Ono Ono Girl's Hula* © 1997 by